YOUTUBE SECRETS
2020

The Ultimate Guide to Increasing your Marketing Influence and Brand Awareness by Growing your YouTube Channel

Aiden Winters

Table of Contents

Introduction

In 2005, an American-Bangladeshi named Jawed Karim uploaded a video of his visit to the zoo.

The video itself was not remarkable. It just features the young man talking about elephants and the length of their trunks.

However, unbeknownst to him, it set out to change the way we would consume content. More specifically, it would shift the dynamics of video content consumption.

No, the video itself did not do that. It was just a video of a regular young man visiting the zoo. An ordinary young man who would later go on to be a multi-millionaire, but that is beside the point.

It was the video sharing platform he uploaded the video to that would create the change.

That platform was YouTube.

Today, we are part of that change. We use YouTube to consume a myriad of content including using the guides and tutorials found on the platform to learn. We watch music videos, movie trailers, game reviews, and sports competitions. Additionally, We can see content on practically any topic, from history to physics to philosophy. We can witness some incredible works of the imagination.

All of this is possible on a platform that boasts the addition of nearly 100 hours of video every minute.

When YouTube launched officially on February 14, 2005, no one could have predicted the direction it would take. It was a real shocker when Google acquired the video-sharing website for about $1.65 billion just a year and a half later.

In today's world of mergers and acquisitions, that acquisition sum sounds paltry. After all, as of 2019, WhatsApp has a price tag of $16 billion attached to it, which Facebook is aiming to meet. However, back then, the amount paid to YouTube was too good to be true.

In fact, industry analysts were somewhat baffled by the acquisition amount. They claimed that Google might have overpaid. Google itself acknowledged the fact that the value of YouTube was not extremely high at that time.

However, decisions were made, and there was no turning back.

While the acquisition might have been questionable then, Google had a clear vision for the video sharing platform. It saw YouTube's popularity soaring above Google Videos (which was Google's own video sharing platform). It saw the advertising and revenue potential of the platform.

These days, the purchase of YouTube by Google is considered one of the best tech acquisitions ever. Industry experts estimate YouTube's current value to be more than $70 billion.

Moreover, to think that all of this began when Chad Hurley, Jawed Karim, and Steven Chen - three PayPal employees - launched a dating site whose primary purpose was for singles to create introductory videos of themselves.

While the founders of YouTube set a new direction for video consumption, Google's purchase was the key to bringing the video sharing platform to the status it enjoys today.

YouTube incorporates a free uploading structure, giving it access to practically anyone on the planet with an internet connection. It features politicians, musicians, gamers, and activists. Anyone of them, given the time and the type of content, can attract millions of viewers.

Let's look at the present situation of YouTube. The channel with the highest subscriber count is a music and entertainment channel managed by a film production and record label company named T-Series. This channel has more than 118 million subscribers. Now you might say, "well, they are a big corporation. It's obvious they can get all those followers."

But guess what channels have occupied the second and third place?

PewDiePie – whose real name is Felix Kjellberg – is a 25-year-old Swede who provides amusing commentary while playing games. His YouTube channel has over 102 million followers, and each of his videos receives millions of views. He currently occupies the second position.

In third place comes a channel focused on children. The channel, named Cocomelon - Nursery Rhymes is run by a small team of independent creators who create 3D animated videos for children. The channel has 65 million subscribers; the fact that it has such a high follower count is proof of the power of YouTube. Even children use the platform!

Let us dive into math territory here. On average, you could earn roughly $1 for every 1,000 views you receive on your video, although that amount could rise to as much as $7. PewDiePie gets an average of 5,000,000 views per video. That's about $5,000 for every video he uploads. Who knew playing video games was so profitable? Think it is about time we brushed the dust off our old consoles.

And what's more, even a children's channel focused on nursery rhymes can earn big bucks on the platform. Let's get back to Cocomelon. This channel has an average of 15 million views for its videos! If we use the same calculations that we had used for PewDiePie's channel, then Cocomelon earns $15,000 per video! Who would have thought children's nursery rhymes were so profitable?! But that is the power of YouTube. It connects you to the audience that you seek, anywhere in the world.

Whether you want to start a cooking class or provide sports commentary, you have a powerful tool to publish your content. If you own a business or are an entrepreneur, you can use YouTube to boost your or your brand's awareness. If you have a home-based company, then you can start publishing content about your niche.

Whatever your aim, you have the means to tell your story, gain influence and build a brand that sells.

Chapter 1:
YouTube and Video Marketing

The Advantages of YouTube Marketing

It is no secret. An impressive number of people have found success through YouTube. If you know names like Justin Bieber, Soulja Boy, and Bo Burnham, then you are aware of the few people who gained fame by posting their videos on YouTube.

Of course, a vast majority of people do not reach the level of fame attained by a select few, but that does not diminish the value of YouTube's potential.

To businesses, video marketing should be a vital component of their inbound marketing strategy. According to Hubspot, nearly 80% of people recollect a video ad viewed in the past month. Also from Hubspot - close to 64% of people are likely to purchase a product online after watching a video.

For individuals, the video platform is an excellent channel for expressing themselves and finding their audience. By focusing on their niche, they might be able to gain a following and create a business model. Eventually, YouTube might become an essential part of their personal branding.

If you are a business, an individual or even part of a group, you can use YouTube to build an effective branding strategy.

But why is YouTube marketing so effective.

Large Audience

According to Alexa, YouTube has the second highest number of visitors after Google. That fact might surprise you a bit as you might have been expecting Facebook to be in the second place (we all know Google has the top spot. Many people set it as the default home page in their browsers after all).

With that much traffic on the site, there is an extraordinary number of views to gain. You are looking at millions of people entering the site to discover information, entertainment, or guidance. Those millions of people are your potential target, and they can help you brand yourself efficaciously as a person or a business.

Create Viral Marketing

When one thinks of viral videos, they think of Keanu Reeves and his 'breathtaking' moment during a video game event, Billie Ellish, the trailer for Avengers: Infinity War or many other favorite content watched and shared by millions.

When it comes to marketing, the idea that we can use a million views to brand ourselves and increase revenue sounds convenient. But that may not be the case in reality.

In viral marketing, we focus less on views and more on how you can encourage your audience to spread information about you. You create an effective strategy where the public shares your content to spread awareness about you or your products and services.

YouTube not only allows you to connect with millions of people but also provides options to share your content. You can embed videos in blogs. You can use shareable links and post them on social platforms. Some websites even allow you to add YouTube videos into their content. You have many ways to share your content and in turn, increase the chances of others resharing your videos.

Create Your Story

A common myth surrounding YouTube is that your content has to be humorous to gain an audience. In reality, you have to create an engaging video. You could talk about anything. From topics that people might consider uninteresting like tax returns and accounting to unusual subjects like the complex structure of a chainsaw. You just need to be well versed in a topic, and YouTube can help you spread the word about you.

The World is Your Audience

Every time the word 'audience' appears, it does not refer to people in your local community, city, or your country. Your audience is anyone who has access to YouTube. Of course, this means that your content could reach people who may not be your target audience. But knowing the fact that you have a global reach is enough to broaden your marketing strategy.

Develop Your SEO

When you perform a Google search, you will often find YouTube videos displayed at the top of the search results. This is an indication that YouTube videos are a powerful addition to your Search Engine Optimization strategy. According to Cisco, global video consumption might amount to nearly 82 percent of the world's IP traffic. This increase might push Google to provide videos even more priority on their search results pages.

As you begin to work on your YouTube channel, a good SEO strategy will allow people to discover you easily. Your brand's visibility increases and you can increase traffic to other sources, such as websites. This becomes particularly useful when you are planning on selling through an online portal.

Understanding Your YouTube Channel

You are now aware of the myriad reasons why you should start a YouTube channel. Whether you would like to brand yourself or the company you manage or work in, YouTube gives you an opportunity to grow your audience, generate traffic, and create an effective marketing strategy.

Before we dive into how you can grow your brand, let us go through the basics first; how to set up your YouTube channel.

But even before that, we might need to touch base on an important subject.

Here are a few points to remember before starting your YouTube channel.

What is your YouTube channel about?

It could be anything; you might decide to talk about the latest news and current affairs. Furthermore, you might want to review the latest tech products and gadgets. You could create a channel for your business. Let us assume that you own a small digital marketing agency. Perhaps you could consider creating a YouTube channel to talk about online marketing, Google ads, social media management, and other topics that focus on digital marketing.

It is essential to narrow down the focus of your channel as it helps you answer a few vital questions:

- What will be the theme of my videos?

- Who will be my target audience?

- Why should people come to my channel to watch my videos?

The above question will help you create videos that you are passionate about and your target audience will enjoy. As you may not have the luxury of time, asking yourself these questions will help you save time in the future, and create a concrete marketing strategy in the present.

What is the frequency of your video uploads?

The frequency of your video uploads refers to the number of videos that you will upload and publish on YouTube.

When you ask yourself this question, think of the response from a realistic point of view. Do you really think you can upload three videos per week? Or are you more comfortable pushing out one video every two weeks?

Here is an important fact to remember: it is not about the number of videos you upload, but the content of those videos that matter. You could publish three videos every week. But if those videos do not interest or engage your audience, then you will have a low number of followers.

What Will Be the Style of My Videos?

YouTube is a visual medium. When people enter the channel, their eyes are drawn towards videos that stimulate their visual senses. If you can serve your audience content and style, then they will consume it enthusiastically. To get your style, you should first work on your visuals, which include the below:

- Captivating titles

- Attractive thumbnails

- Consistency in your visuals

Additionally, you should think about where you would like to record the video. Will it be inside your home? How are the lighting levels? If you are going to comment or speak in your videos, do you have the right audio equipment?

What Equipment Do I Require?

Once you figure out the overall content and style of your channel, you need to figure out how you are going to capture your content. To start creating high-quality videos, you need the right hardware. Now, this might make you check your bank balance, hoping you have enough financial resources to spend on your first equipment. But you really do not have to splurge a lot of money getting what you need.

Here is a list of equipment you might require:

Camera: Do not spend on a DSLR if you cannot. You could use your smartphone camera, provided it can record high-quality videos. You could record directly via your computer or laptop webcam. Once you get your channel rolling, you can think of investing in better video capturing devices.

Microphone: You could use the microphone that comes with your mobile device or computer to record your voice, but I honestly recommend getting an external audio recording device. Do not worry, you can find the market littered with inexpensive microphones.

Tripod: No one likes a shaky cam. Unless you are recording the next Jason Bourne movie. Get yourself a tripod if you are using a mobile device. This is not just for keeping the device stable but aligning it to get the right camera angle. For desktop computers, you can skip the tripod purchase.

Green Screen: This tool may not be essential, but it depends on the kind of content you are recording. Using a green screen, you can add backgrounds to your videos. You can either purchase a green screen in the market or search YouTube (see what I did there?) to find out how to make one at home.

With all of the above points in mind, let us move on to the next part; creating your YouTube channel.

Is There Any Information That I Should Keep in Mind?

As of November 2019, YouTube has updated its terms and conditions. Under the updated terms, YouTube is no longer under any obligation to serve or host content. But, what exactly does that mean? The entire phrasing is rather vague. That's because it covers a whole range of topics, but the most important one that creators should be concerned about is the idea of hosting their videos on the platform.

For years, there has been criticism about the platform. Some video creators have openly told the platform that it should primarily support creators and not be biased in any way. Others feel that the platform should start curbing the content that is created on its platform. In other words, there are people who are arguing for tighter restrictions.

Most important to remembers is that even though YouTube is a fairly open platform, it does not mean that it is under any mandate to keep videos. It can remove videos if they violate certain terms and conditions without giving further details. What has many people concerned about this update is that YouTube can terminate a creator's access to his or her YouTube and Gmail account if it feels that rules or regulations have been violated. And what conditions dictate such violations? Apparently, those are decided by YouTube itself.

While this might sound concerning, it is important to remember that it also offers a greater level of security on the platform. This rule allows the platform to remove any explicit content. Think about it this way. Imagine that you have created a kids channel and you have family-friendly content. Now imagine that an advertisement pops up in your channel that contains some rather questionable messages that are definitely not appropriate for children or minors. What do you do in such scenarios?

With YouTube having your back, you'll know that your channel is protected and that you can reach out to your audience with relative peace of mind.

Creating Your YouTube Channel

This is the exciting part. Well, one of the exciting parts.

If you are thinking that getting a YouTube channel is going to be challenging, then you can relax. I am going to break down the process into simple steps. You ready? Let's go ahead and get started.

Basics. Which Means, You Need A Google Account

This is the exciting part. Well, one of the exciting parts.

If you are thinking that getting a YouTube channel is going to be challenging, then you can relax. I am going to break down the process into simple steps. You ready? Let's get started.

Basics. Which Means, You Need A Google Account

The first thing you have to do is sign in to your YouTube account. If you have Gmail, then your login details serve as your YouTube access. If you do not have Gmail, merely create an account for yourself and login to YouTube using your email's username and password.

Once you have logged into YouTube, follow the below steps:

- On the top right corner of the page, click on your profile icon

- In the drop-down menu that follows, click on the settings icon (should resemble the universal symbol of a cogwheel)

- When you reach the "Account Settings" page, make sure you are in the "Overview" tab.

- You will spot the "Create a channel" option under "Account Information." Click it!

- You will now notice the option to create a channel using your personal name, or you can alternatively create a business channel.

- We'll go ahead and choose the business option (or did you forget the name of this book?), which should appear to you as "Use a business or other name."

- The next step involves naming your channel and choosing your channel category.

- Pick a name for your channel. You could pick a name that represents what your channel focuses on, or you could use your real name. Eventually, your YouTube channel will be your brand.

- Next, pick a category. There are four categories to choose from, and these are "Product or Brand," "Company Institution or Organization," "Arts, Entertainment or

Sports," and "Other." Pick the option that best fits your YouTube. I recommend avoiding choosing "Other" unless you strongly feel that your channel does not fit in the other three options.

- When you are ready, click the "Done" button.

That's it! You have taken your first steps towards creating your YouTube channel. Let us continue further.

The Art of the Channel

The next step is to create your channel art. No need to worry if you are not a graphic designer, there a myriad of different ways to outsource the work to someone for a relatively inexpensive price point. I will cover how you can do this in a later section of this book, but for the sake of congruence, let's move forward. The channel art image is YouTube's version of the favorite "Cover Photo" that you use on Facebook. It is a strip of graphics added to your channel to make it recognizable and give it a little personality.

Your channel art is relevant because people use it to recognize you. It is also a way to brand your channel and give it personality. You should ideally use a customized image as the channel art; this image could show your area of expertise or could feature you in it. Even more, you could add text on the image or merely choose to use graphics to show your channel's focus.

Let's use an example to give you inspiration. Head over to YouTube and look at the channel of gaming news presenter Yong. His channel, YongYea has a cover photo that includes his unique signature along with the words "News. Reviews. Discussions." You can also see an animated image of Yong's face on the right side of the cover photo. The channel art showcases Yong's passion for gaming and his mission to bring gaming related news and information to his audience. But does each and every channel art have to include words and descriptions? Not really.

Let's take a look at another channel, Mental Floss. The channel's art includes its name in the center of the picture. The rest of the image is composed of grid boxes of various shapes. In each box, you will find an image, such as a butterfly, a telescope, a rocket, the radiation zone sign, and so on. The pictures are all displayed in pastel colors. This shows the channel's focus; science and facts. But they want to present their content in a fun way, which is maybe why they have used pastel colors to showcase the lightheartedness of the channel.

Similarly, think about what your channel will focus on. If you are a business, then ask yourself how you can represent your business in a graphic.

When you are ready, you should take note of the channel art dimensions to create the perfect image. YouTube recommends using an image that is 2,560 pixels wide and 1,440 pixels tall.

However, different devices have different size requirements. Here is an image to help you with YouTube's channel art dimensions:

For the audio version of this book, I will attach a PDF for reference.

Figure 1. Google. YouTube channel art image size guidelines [Image]. Retrieved from
https://support.google.com/youtube/answer/2972003?hl=en

Here are a few points to remember about channel art:

- The minimum file dimensions should be 2,048 pixels wide and 1,152 pixels tall.

- For text and logos, the minimum safe area is 1,546 pixels wide and 423 pixels tall.

- Regarding the minimum width, it should be 2,560 pixels wide and 423 pixels tall. Using this size, your "safe area" will usually be visible regardless of the size of the screen.

- The image file size should be no more than 4MB.

So according to the guide, if you use an image sized 2,048 pixels by 1,152 pixels, then your image might fit a television screen perfectly. However, it would be best if you thought about how the art fits other devices as well, such as a mobile phone or desktop computer. Using the above image and size recommendations as guides, find out how to create the ideal channel art.

Adding Your Channel Art

Once you have your channel art ready, it is time to add it to your channel.

- Head over to your profile icon and click it. This time, click on the "Creator Studio" option.

- In the next page, make sure that you are under the "Dashboard" tab.

- Once there, you should see the "View Channel" link right below your channel name. Click on this option.

- You will now notice your channel's page. Here you should be able to see an "Add channel art" button superimposed on a blank cover background. Click on this option.

- At this point, you will be able to choose from photos you have saved or pick a picture from a gallery. Alternatively, you can upload an image from your computer. Go right ahead and select that option.

- After the upload is complete, you get the option to crop your image. On the crop screen, you will be able to see how the image appears on various devices. Work with your image until you find the ideal position and check to see if you are happy with how it performs in multiple formats. Using the "Devices preview" button, you can check the alignment of your image on various platforms. When you are ready to confirm your image, click on the "Select" button and you are done.

- You are now the proud owner of beautiful channel art!

With your channel art, you might be satisfied with the results of your first upload, or you might decide to use another. You could also choose to change your channel art in the future, perhaps to a better one. Whatever your reasons for changing your channel art, you can edit it using a few easy steps.

Just like the process involved in uploading your image, head over to your profile icon and click on Creator Studio, navigate to your Dashboard and choose the "View Channel" option. At your channel page, you will notice an edit button on top of your channel art. Click this button and choose another image. It is as simple as that.

Adding Your Profile Icon

With all this talk about profile icon, there should be a way to change it right? Of course, there is!

To add an image to your profile icon, head back to your channel page (where you changed your channel art). You will see an edit option over your profile image. Click on that option and choose an image for your profile.

- You can use JPG, BMP, or PNG image formats for your profile icon. You can also use a non-animated GIF for the image.

- Image size should be 800 pixels wide and 800 pixels tall.

Linking Your Channel

You can add links to your channel that will sit atop your channel art. These links are a great way to drive traffic to other platforms, such as your website, Facebook page, Instagram account or your Twitter account.

Linking channels proves effective to get your community together. If you have other social media accounts, then spreading awareness about those accounts allow your YouTube subscribers to join them. Adding social media links increase your channel's visibility and gives you the opportunity to connect with your audience in multiple ways.

Time for an example.

Let us assume that you have a Facebook account where you are planning to promote your merchandise. You want more people to reach your Facebook page and check out all the cool stuff you have. Apart from using social advertising, adding your link on your YouTube profile gives you or your brand that extra level of exposure.

So let us go ahead add those links for you.

- Once again, head over to your channel page where you can change your channel art and profile icon. You will notice a "Subscribe" button below your channel art. Next to the button is a cogwheel icon (wonder what that is eh?). Click on that icon.

- A pop-up will appear before you that shows your channel's settings.

- On this pop-up, you will spot an option that says, "Customize the layout of your channel." Turn it on if it is not in the on position already.

- After this, head back to your channel page, and you will notice the "Edit Links" option on your channel art.

- Go ahead and click that.

- You will be taken to a separate page where you will be able to add links. Here, you can choose exactly how many links will appear on your channel. You should notice this: Overlay first [number] custom links on channel art. The [number] is a drop-down menu allowing you to choose the number of visible links on your channel. Go ahead and select your preferred number option.

- Below that, you can add all the social links you want to add.

- The end. That is all there is to it!

Create Your Channel Trailer

Your account is now ready to reveal all its glorious content to the world. However, before that, here is a suggestion from my end. If you have entered a YouTube channel, you will often notice a video that auto-plays upon your entry. This video is called a "channel trailer."

Again, you can have this made by a talented professional via outsourcing, which I will cover a bit later.

A channel trailer is a great way to introduce your audience to your YouTube channel. You want them to know why they should invest their time on your channel and eventually, subscribe to your content. A trailer gives you the opportunity to communicate that message in some creative ways. The trailer plays as soon as the viewer enters your YouTube channel.

Your trailer should be concise, clear, and should get straight to the point. It can be funny, informative, motivational, or educational. It should represent you and give an idea of what the audience can expect from your channel.

You might think that you should probably create a hilarious video that will have your audience gasping for breath from laughter. That sounds good. Even more, if your content is not going to be comedic - or light-hearted - then you have placed false expectations on your audience. That only tends to work against you. People will refuse to return to your channel because they did not get what they came for.

So do not worry about being funny. Think about being genuine. Make this channel about you, and if the audience feels your content is riveting and engaging, then they will come to your channel in droves.

To set any video as your channel trailer, follow the below steps:

- Make sure you have toggled on the "Customize the layout of your channel" option. Refer to "Linking Your Channel" section to see how you can do this.

- Go ahead and navigate to your channel's page. Once there, you have the option to upload a video to your channel. Upload your trailer if you haven't done so already.

- Once the upload is complete, head back to your channel's page. You will notice the video sitting under the tab "For returning subscribers."

- Head over to the "For new visitors" tab.

- Once there, click on the "+ Channel trailer" button.

- Select your video from the list of uploaded videos. Alternatively, you can even enter the URL of your YouTube video.

- Once done, click save.

You now have a trailer for your YouTube channel. Feels pretty awesome, doesn't it?

Getting Someone to Create Your YouTube Channel

I have given you all the necessary steps to start creating your YouTube channel. However, there might be situations when time may not be on your side. You could have other engagements, or you might find the process of creating a YouTube channel complicated. It is understandable to have the feeling that you do not want to make a single mistake on your YouTube channel, especially before you even start uploading your first few videos.

In that case, you can hire someone to work on your channel. In my opinion, the part where you might need someone with skills is when you are working on your channel art. Not everyone can work with graphics, and a graphic designer could have better input on your channel art design.

Whatever task you would like completed, you can make use of freelancers. It is quite easy to find freelancers, especially when portals are providing you freelancing services. I recommend using Upwork.com, but you have other options such as Freelancer and Fiverr.

There are portals where you can look for remote assistance from across the globe. Head over to outsourcely.com, fiverr.com, remotelyawesomejobs.com or golance.com to get someone to work on your channel art.

You could also make use of your local online classifieds. A lot of them are usually free, and you can get in touch with someone skilled through an online ad.

Look to your friends or family for help. Perhaps you might already know someone who has the skills and experience you are looking for.

Get a Team

Nowadays, many YouTubers are looking to be part of a team. You might find channels that are managed by more than one person, and sometimes by a group of up to five people. If you think that you can get your friends, family, or anyone else to work with you on the channel, then that would be a bonus. But make sure that you have explained the details of your channel to the person or people who are going to be joining you. That will help them figure out how to plan out the timing of their posts.

In many cases, you can even work with someone who has editing and graphic design skills. This will help you immensely since you can bring in someone who can present your video in an exciting and entertaining manner.

If you look at numerous channels, you might notice friends, family members, or even couples sitting in front of a camera and presenting their content. If you do not want to spend a lot of time on editing, then you can use this format to easily create content. Plus, looking into the camera is a great way to engage with the audience.

If you are going to have a team, then you can have someone work on all the edits and other special effects for your videos. This person doesn't have to be in the videos themselves. He or she will be working behind the scenes to make your content look special.

Making it Big

If you are a regular visitor on YouTube (which you should be at this point), you might notice a lot of big names on the platform. Whenever you require some inspiration, you have only to look at how these YouTube personalities made their mark.

Moreover, where they are right now.

That said, let me introduce you to a few of them.

PewDiePie

You might probably know him for his running commentary on the games that he plays. His expletive-ridden videos are watched all over the world. However, before he could be an internet sensation, he had another remarkable job.

Would you believe it if I told you that Felix Kjellberg, the YouTube personality with the highest follower count, used to sell hot dogs?

That is right; before Kjellberg could gain more than 102 million followers, he had modest beginnings. The man was known to enjoy games tremendously during his childhood. Furthermore, as Felix grew older, his passion for games merely intensified, that said, he spent many hours in his bedroom and internet cafes gaming as much as possible.

He opened his first YouTube channel in 2006 and named it PewDie. However, soon, he lost interest in the channel, eventually forgetting the password of his YouTube account.

In 2010, he set up another account, this time naming it PewDiePie (the name we are all familiar with), and the rest, as they say, is YouTube history.

According to Forbes, Felix earned a whopping $15 million in 2018. That and he launched his book titled "This Book Loves You."

So let this rag to riches – or hot dogs to YouTube channel to be more precise – story inspire you. The only limit that you place on your channel is the one that might come from you.

You could be on the Forbes list as well. Moreover, perhaps push out your own book.

Markiplier

Mark Edward Fischbach, or Markiplier, as he is known to his community (and which is also the name his channel) is a YouTuber who has proven that having fun and constantly innovating your content creates a loyal fan base.

Markiplier has considerable influence on the platform. In November 2019, his channel came under attack because of YouTube's privacy and security policy. He features live streaming and a new interactive video for his followers. When his followers began reacting to his channel, they got their own channels and accounts blocked by YouTube. This error was not caused because of any problems caused by the followers. Rather, YouTube's algorithm had mistaken the activities of the followers of Markiplier's channel as harmful.

The next day, Markiplier addressed the issue. Within 12 hours, YouTube's team had personally gotten in touch with him to resolve the situation.

Markiplier started working on his channel in 2012. During his early years, he was known for playing video games and reacting to them. He would often play the scariest horror games in a darkened room and then react to the game's many frightening moments. Over the years, his content evolved to focus on various comedy topics and sketches.

In fact, his creativity is what drives fans towards his channel. In mid-November 2019, he created a channel named Unus Annus (taken from Latin and which translates to "one year") along with fellow YouTuber Ethan Nestor. The unique concept of the channel is that it will release one video every day for an entire year. At the end of that year, all the videos and content on that channel will be deleted permanently. The focus of each video will be to create comedy content featuring unique ideas. For example, one of the videos shows Mark and Ethan creating their own sensory deprivation tank and using it. Within just 3 days of the channel's creation, the videos had garnered an average of 1.3 million views.

Jenna Marbles

Among the female celebrities of YouTube, no one has quite the influence that Jenna Marbles does.

This comedian has more than 18 million followers on YouTube and counting.

However, before she could reach her level of fame, she had to find her spark first. She uploaded her first video in 2010, which was titled "Charles Franklin Marbles is a Sad, Sad Man."

Since then, she began frequently adding videos to her YouTube account. While they did receive numerous views, none of them got her massive recognition. It wasn't until she uploaded her video, "How to trick people into thinking you're good looking," that she found herself propelled into YouTube stardom.

Her videos show her wacky personality as she comments and muses about different topics. She uses minimal props as her focus is on what she has to say to the audience.

As with the other two YouTube personalities that I talked about, Jenna made it into Forbes, with the magazine estimating her earnings to be in the range of several millions of dollars.

Fear of the Unknown

There are many reasons why you would want to start your own

YouTube channel. Also, there are many reasons why you wouldn't.

While starting a YouTube channel might sound easy, much goes into that decision. More specifically, you have to convince one person that it will be taking the most effort into making the channel great; you.

Coming up with the idea for your YouTube channel does not seal the fate of your channel in stone. Implementing your idea and turning your plans into actions decides what happens to your channel. Every single step you take to create your channel might convince you about the futility of keeping the channel running.

You might get bombarded with a dozen questions.

Does this sound like the right thing to do? Should I even both with a YouTube channel? What will happen one year from the day I create my YouTube account? Will I be able to find an audience for my content? What if I somehow manage to embarrass myself?

Let me try to alleviate your doubts and apprehensions.

Time and Hard Work

Once you create your YouTube channel, you need to put in your time and effort into it. No channel has gained instant popularity. Most of the famous YouTubers that you know of have tried and tested their content repeatedly. They had to keep at it until they hit the jackpot with that one content that got them the recognition they needed. Similarly, you might need to put your focus, patience, and effort, and maintain consistency in your content. That is how you can get your channel to the position you have aimed for.

Now you might be wondering: wait just a minute. Why is this author talking about time, effort, and patience? I thought he was supposed to motivate me into working on the channel. Now I feel like I might want to avoid going on YouTube altogether!

On the contrary, I am showing you that working on your YouTube channel is like working on any other endeavor in your life. If you plan to start your business, you know you would have to put in hard work to propel it to greater heights. You know the challenges you might face while bringing your company plans to fruition. That said, eventually, you might find yourself reaping the fruits of your hard work.

The same principles that apply to businesses apply to YouTube as well. In actuality, in today's digital world, it is safe to say that YouTube is a business.

There are no extraordinary tricks you can use. There are no easy shortcuts you can take. Every YouTuber had been in your place, figuring out their content and consistently working on their channel.

Which is why you can reach the same level that these YouTube influencers have achieved. You have an equal opportunity as they had and you have every possibility to make it just as big on YouTube as well.

Influential

Being on YouTube means having influence. People come to you because they believe in your content. They trust your voice and take inspiration from you. They look to you for education, entertainment or even motivation. As soon as they find what they are looking for, they want more of it. They follow you and actively begin watching your content. Soon, they might inform their friends and acquaintances of your channel, who in turn might refer your channel to others and so on.

You might be featured in online blogs and articles. A publication agency might write a piece on your channel.

Slowly, your influence grows. You might reach a point where you are either the best content provider of your niche or among the top YouTube channels who provide similar content.

This level of influence can, in turn, be used to market yourself, your brand (if you have one), or even create your own personal line of products and services. For many YouTubers, their channel or real names are their brands as well.

Significant influence and recognition are among the many rewards you may receive for all the efforts you put into your YouTube channel. As I had mentioned before, you start on the same playing field as many others.

What could differentiate you from other content creators is your style, persistence, and consistency.

Ripe Market

You might think that other YouTube channels have already explored your ideas thoroughly. However, take the time to browse through YouTube. Watch videos of the content that you like.

You might notice new faces and new channels where once they did not exist.

New channels pop up all the time because people want to consume more content; they look for novelty; they look for variety. According to Alexa, that estimate daily pageviews per visitor on YouTube is five pages. That is more than Facebook's estimated pageviews of three per visitor!

That is five pieces of content that each person might consume on YouTube.

With millions of visitors from around the world, you have myriad of opportunities to be noticed. So do not think about whether your content might have an audience. Think about the content itself.

Uncertain Where to Start

Not sure who your target audience is? No problem. You do not have to figure out everything at the beginning.

Finding your audience takes time. You could gain a loyal following within your city. Alternatively, you might become popular on the other side of the globe. Where your content takes you is something you might not quickly or easily figure out.

If you are looking for a place to start, think about people close to you.

You could start with your local community. You could invite your friends and family to follow you. Let them be your critique; allow them to form honest opinions about your channel. Once you receive their feedback, show your content to other people in your area. Post your content on your Facebook.

Through small strategies, you can begin to grow your YouTube audience and find out whom you should target. You might get insights on the location of your largest concentration of followers.

YouTube provides you incredible analytics tools and insights to measure the performance and reach of your videos. You have many ways to know more about your visitors. Such as, what video did they watch the most, which video received the least views, and where is the majority of your audience from? How much time did they spend on your videos?

You can find spectacular insights that allow you to narrow down the focus on your content.

Personal Branding

Your channel is all about you. It helps you market yourself in one of the best ways possible. You instantly reach out to so many audiences and open up many opportunities for business or revenue streams. Let us assume that you own a small business. A YouTube channel helps bring you into the limelight and in turn, gives your business exposure.

If you are an individual, you get to focus on content that you are passionate about and create an identity for yourself. Your level of passion is key to eventually opening doors and reaching out to other businesses, brands, or agencies. You might become part of collaborations, which might create opportunities for even more content.

Through your efforts, you can build a reputation for yourself. This reputation might give you access to media networks, publications, businesses, and influencers.

When you slowly begin to gain a reputation, you can sell your brand.

The possibilities you can achieve through YouTube are aplenty. The only trick is to work on your content.

Chapter 2:
Content is the Name of the Game

You are by now fully aware of how influential YouTube is. You have also started plotting about the nitty-gritty details of creating your own YouTube channel. That said, you more than understand that the market is ripe for more content. Hence, you are about to take your first step forward.

But wait, what if you are finding it somewhat challenging to figure out what kind of content you would like to focus on?

Maybe you are looking for the right subject matter or the right style.

In that case, worry not my fellow would-be YouTubers. I got your covered.

We will now look at what kind of content you could work with. We will get into the details of posting on YouTube, discovering when to post and the frequency in which you should post.

Niches That Work best for YouTube

As I mentioned earlier, starting a YouTube channel involves a fair bit of work. If you have already figured out your content style and matter, then you are almost ready to get started on your YouTube channel. If you are still pondering the intricate details of your content, then perhaps I might be able to help you with your problem.

In this chapter, I am going to inform you about content niches that work well on YouTube. After all, you are going to be consistent with your content. You might as well choose the niche that works for you best.

There is an important point that I would like to bring up here. Creating a YouTube channel just to earn money might not allow you to create quality content. Video creation is a lot of work, and if you do not enjoy what you do, you might give up on your channel sooner than you think.

When you love what you do, you work twice as hard on your content to make sure your audience enjoy it.

And that is how you eventually turn your channel profitable.

Now that we have gotten that out of the way, let us dive into some popular YouTube content niches.

Gaming

You might think that PewDiePie is my favorite YouTube channel. While he has incredible content, in reality, he is an excellent example to follow. Unsurprisingly, he will be making an appearance as an example in this section as well. Felix and other gaming vloggers like Markiplier, Laymen Gaming, and ACG are extremely popular on YouTube.

There are many ways you can tackle this niche.

You can create game reviews, where you walk through some of the highs and lows of the latest video game releases. You can choose to review games released for a specific console, or you can go ahead and discuss a wide array of video games. For example, you could solely focus on PlayStation 4 video games or expand to include PC and Nintendo gaming.

You could have fun with games as well. This involves showing your reactions while playing horror games, noticing some crazy features of games, or just trying something that no one else has.

You could review the gaming industry as a whole, talking about the latest technology that is already available and will be made available. You can discuss topics that might interest the community at large. For example, do you think a specific gaming manufacturer has broken the rules because of certain actions? Do prefer a particular type of trend to another? Should people pay exorbitant prices to get additional content?

You can also create channels where people can watch you play a particular game and see you react to many of the gaming moments. There are channels that are focused on understanding gaming mechanics and helping people play video games better.

Nowadays, the gaming space has become more crowded. You have plenty of gaming focused channels, each offering news, video game plays, advice, secrets, and many other types of content. The best part is that despite the growing number of channels focused on gaming, you still have opportunities to create an audience for yourself.

YouTube Channels for Inspiration

- ACG

- Laymen Gaming

- UberHaxorNova

- AfroSenju

Beauty

The makeup market brings out newer products, and people are eager to know what to get.

With a beauty channel, you can give people recommendations

and form your own opinions on a variety of makeup products. You will be their go-to-guide for anything related to beauty.

Additionally, most makeup vlogs involve tutorials. You can take inspiration for tutorials from various sources. You can get started on ideas that you are confident sharing on camera and start putting your own touch to your content.

You could provide makeup tips for a lot of occasions and uses. A few examples to highlight here are makeup tutorials for removing dark circles, tips to get ready in five minutes in the morning, and ways to add blush to your face.

There are many ways to work with makeup products as well. You can form content based on that. For example, you could show people that a makeup case can double as a storage unit for small items like pens, cards, and keys. Bet you might not have thought that!

There are plenty of ways to plant your roots in the world of makeup. However, as makeup often involves looking good on camera, make sure that you have a high-quality capturing device and proper lighting.

Most importantly, makeup involves many details. Do not hesitate to research into a subject before creating a video about it.

All you need to do is find a niche for yourself and stick to it.

YouTube Channels for Inspiration

- jeffreestar

- NikkieTutorials

- Zoella

Children's Shows and Nursery Rhymes

Remember Talking Tom? This character was part of a mobile app where you record your voice and the character on the screen replays your voice in a humorous way. Guess what? He has his own animated series!

  Typically, you might imagine that people who plan to create a cartoon series might approach Cartoon Network or some of the other popular TV channels. At best, they might think of making a deal with Netflix or Hulu.

Not these days.

The creators started their channel named after the character; Talking Tom. As of November 2019, the channel has over 25 million subscribers.

When the creators of Talking Tom realized the potential of YouTube to reach an audience of any age group, they decided to take advantage of it. In fact, did you know that YouTube has a special format called "YouTube Kids" where all the content is safe for the little ones? Think about it. The idea that a group of creators started creating content for kids and those content became such a massive influence that YouTube decided to create a safe space for them, where kids are not bombarded with mature content and advertising.

Are you skilled in animation? Why not create a 3D children's channel like Cocomelon? In fact, one of their popular videos features animated toddlers singing along to the "Baby Shark" melody. As of November 2019, that video has received 1.4 billion views and has single-handedly generated millions of dollars of revenue for the channel.

Don't have skills in animation? Not to worry. YouTube features a host of kids channels who create family-friendly content.

Perhaps you could take inspiration from a few of them. For instance, Ryan is an adorable 6-year old who is the star of the YouTube channel Ryan's ToysReview. He checks out cool toys and gives his feedback about them. He has 9.4 million subscribers and collective video views of over 16.5 trillion!

Don't want to focus on toys? No problem! Check out EvanTubeHD, the channel hosted by 12-year old Evan who reviews toys, but also focuses on creating challenges and incredible science experiments. And guess what? Business Insider reported that Evan earns a cool $1.3 million a year. Imagine telling someone that you know a 12-year old millionaire who has his own show.

YouTube Channels for Inspiration

- Seven Awesome Kids
- Ethan Gamer
- babyteeth4
- B2cuteCupcakes

Food and Restaurant

Orson Welles famously quoted, "Ask not what you can do for your country. Ask what's for lunch."

I think he was onto something there.

There is nothing more tantalizing than watching food videos and salivating over some lip-smacking dishes.

Food videos are great for two reasons:

- People enjoy spending countless hours finding inspiration for food

- You get to eat while you shoot your video!

For your food channel, you could focus on cooking. Perhaps you could create delicious recipes or highlight easily to make dishes.

If you are not confident about your cooking skills, you can try other ideas for your channel. You may have your videos point out some incredible tips people can use in their kitchen while traveling, or for other purposes.

You can be a restaurant reviewer. Most restaurants might not allow large cameras within their premises. However, you just require a handheld device (it is also convenient to have smaller equipment as you can conveniently eat and record the video) and you can start capturing your video.

There are plenty of opportunities to try out local hotspots. Or if you are feeling adventurous, plan your video around food destinations. You can talk about the cuisines from around the world, combining culture, history, and of course, food.

One of the best parts about focusing on food is that you do not have to compete with international vloggers. This is because you can gain a large audience in your home base (a.k.a. your city or country).

YouTube Channels for Inspiration

- Rosanna Pansino

- Epic Meal Time

- Tipsy Bartender

- How to Cook That

Tech and Gadgets

People love to make informed decisions about technology, hardware, and gadgets. No one likes to splurge on something they may later regret purchasing. Which is why consumers look to experts to guide them the way. You could also have consumers looking for inspiration on a specific gadget.

Whatever their requirements, you can give them the info they need through your channel.

The tech and gadget community on YouTube has heavy competition. This is because it is not easy to build trust among audiences. They need to know that you are well informed and you know what you are talking about. However, if you can give the audience detailed, well-informed, and entertaining content, you can raise the popularity of your channel faster than most niches.

This is because when people begin trusting you, they readily share your content and recommend it to others.

With this niche, you should have the ability to break down complex features and mechanics. With your capabilities, you can focus on either product reviews or comparisons between two items of the same category. You could take the thing for a test run or put the gadget under a stress test to gauge its limits.

You can use technology in many different ways. For example, did you know that you could use your blender to make pancakes?

These DIY tips and tech hacks are quite popular among audiences and are easily shareable (given that people across the globe might use some of the gadgets that you focus on).

YouTube Channels for Inspiration

- MKHBD

- SoldierKnowsBest

- TechSmartt

- 5-minute Crafts - they are not solely technology focused. Their content is based on sharing DIY techniques. However, they sometimes use gadgets to get their results. Plus, if you would like to use DIY content for your channel, you can take inspiration from 5-minute crafts to see how to make the video.

Opinions

These days, it seems like everyone has an opinion about everything. And you probably do as well. If you feel like you can provide opinions on various subjects, then you can create a YouTube channel of your own as well.

But be warned. According to YouTube's updated regulations in 2019, the mention of certain words might get your channel flagged by the platform. If your channel is flagged, then you might get demonetized and the video will stop earning any revenue from the advertisers. The most obvious words to avoid are profanity, although mildly-profane words such as 'damn,' 'hell,' and 'bugger' are currently accepted. Words such as 'gay' and 'lesbian' are likely to get your video demonetized. This of course caught the attention of the LGBTQ community, who had petitioned to YouTube to remove such restrictions.

Keep checking your local newspaper or news channel to discover if there are any topics that are trending. Based on the trending topics, certain words could be flagged by YouTube's guidelines. For example, as of November 2019, you cannot used words such as "abuse," "crime," and "Nazi."

A list of words that are banned is never going to be 100% accurate. YouTube constantly adds or removes words based on the political, social, and economic scenarios around the world. In October, due to news reports about police shootings, the phrase '911' was also added to the flagged words list. If you look through recent videos where people use the three-digit number, then you might also notice advertisements being played on the channel. That shows that YouTube has officially taken 911 off its flagged words list.

When creating channels based on opinion, expect strong comments from the opposition. Often, it is said that those who create opinion channels should have a "thick skin," meaning creators should have a high resistance to criticism and be able to reply or respond with strong counter-arguments. At the same time, opinions can always get you on YouTube's radar, which might not always be a good thing for you.

YouTube Channels for Inspiration

- Nerdrotic

- penguinz0

- Like Stories of Old

- Russell Brand

Health and Fitness

People want to lead healthy lives. However, people may not want to spend time and money on expensive consultations. Their solution? The internet.

Even on the internet, videos give visual information, making it easier for the audience to digest the content. They prefer video content over a written one. Which is why, many people seek out health and fitness tips, information, and recommendations on YouTube.

When you focus on the health and fitness niche, you are helping people better their lives. You could talk about fitness routines at the gym and help people get started on their workout goals. You can include content about healthy exercises people can perform in the comfort of their own homes. You could also talk about recommendations for a healthy diet. When creating any content, you can combine your tips and suggestions with facts about the body that your audience might not know. This makes you sound knowledgeable and that in turn improves people's confidence in you. It establishes you as an authority figure in that specific niche if you demonstrate a vast amount of knowledge. This builds trust very fast.

You could switch to animated characters for your channel as well, though I recommend appearing in front of the camera yourself. People like to have a role model when looking at health and fitness videos.

YouTube Channels for Inspiration

- Jordan Yeoh Fitness

- Dr. Sam Robbins

- Healthy Life

- The Fitness Marshall

Travel

Around the world in a YouTube channel; that might probably be the theme of your content. People are curious to know about the world. Some of them might not have the opportunity to travel and would like to explore the globe through video content. Others are probably looking for inspiration on their next travel destination. For some others, it is a matter of curiosity; they want to know more about different places, people, cultures, and histories.

Your channel could be the go-to point for travel related content. If you are able to, you could explore the many destinations of the world, giving your audiences glimpses of its sights, people, food, culture, and history. You could even blend your travel content with food, turning your channel into a food and travel experience. This could appeal to a broader audience.

Because you will be traveling to several destinations, you might require advance planning to get everything in order. You might have to book the right hotel and see if the hotel has WiFi connectivity, in case you want to upload videos. You might have to arrange for transportation or even a tour guide.

You might need extra equipment to capture a few shots. For example, you might be experiencing white-water rafting. But you cannot use just any camera to capture your adventure. You might need a waterproof camera or an "action camera", such as a GoPro that gives your audience a better perspective.

While travel content involves a lot of work, you have the benefit of combining the joy of traveling with the idea of turning your YouTube channel into a brand.

YouTube Channels for Inspiration

- Fun For Louis

- Sonia's Travels

- Vagabrothers

- The Planet D

- Hopscotch The Globe

Fashion and Style

People love to look good, and you can help them with that. With your fashion channel, you can introduce people to the latest trends, accessories, tips, and more.

The best part of this niche is that you do not necessarily have to be an expert. Different people might have different opinions on a sense of fashion. What you can do is create a unique perspective on the latest wear to inspire people.

You could introduce your audience to various styles that they can use for different occasions. These styles could be summer wear, formal dresses or suits, casual clothing, and more. You could talk about accessories that include jewelry, watches, shoes, and a whole lot of others.

Fashion can also include DIY tips, where you can take a piece of clothing and show unique ways of wearing it. Here is one. Ever had the zippers of your jeans constantly loosening? Well, just use a keyring! Take the ring and loop it around the jeans button and the zipper. It is that simple.

Did that tip just make you go, "I did not know that. That is definitely interesting. Should I give it a try"?

You can get that same reaction from your audience. And if you manage to grab their interest long enough, you gain followers who are more than happy to share your content.

The fashion niche does involve more competition. But do not let that deter you from creating your own unique content. The trick is to understand what you can contribute to this category.

Because everybody's story and unique style has a unique audience specific to them. Why not you?

YouTube Channels for Inspiration

- The Notorious KIA

- Dulce Candy

- Annalee and Jesse

- Rclbeauty101

Animals and Pets

Who does not love cat videos? To garner millions of views, people capture our feline friends committing unnatural acts of hilarity. You can see cats standing on two legs, reacting to a horror movie, or even walking down the road as though they own the street.

You can capture animals and pets in many ways. The possibilities are quite literally, endless.

Your channel could focus on taking care of pets. How do you keep them healthy? What are the best ways to entertain them? What kinds of food should you avoid giving them?

Your videos could feature you visiting pet stores and interacting with pet experts. You can throw in interesting facts about animals and show in-depth knowledge about their anatomy.

Perhaps creating funny videos involving your pets or animals could be what you are looking for.

One of the benefits of starting a pet channel is that often, you might just capture animals in an act spontaneously. This means using any recording device you have near you. But this also means that many others are capturing their pets on camera using inexpensive recording devices (just search dog videos on YouTube, and you'll see what I mean).

Also, make sure you are not allergic to any animal as this allows you to work with many furry creatures.

Make sure that you are being careful when handling animals or pets. The YouTube community is strong and if they notice instances of animal abuse or harm, they can easily report your content. This usually leads to an investigation and if it has been discovered that you are guilty of what the community has reported you for, then you might face a permanent ban. Now this doesn't necessarily mean that you are a person capable of harming animals; but you might not think something is harmful until you start getting reported by the community. Stay on the safe side and ensure that you are creating harmless content.

YouTube Channels for Inspiration

- Hope For Paws

- Vet Ranch

- Elli Di Pets

- Drew Lynch

- Cooking With Dog (This is an interesting concept where the food category is combined with the animals and pets niche.)

Movies and TV Shows

Film and television lovers can start a YouTube channel focusing on their interests. You could talk about all the latest entertainment news on the big and small screen.

Most people imagine that a movie channel should only feature reviews and ratings. But you can create something unique with your channel.

You could have your channel focus on understanding complex movies, dissecting their narratives and giving people more clarity on the story. You could even keep your discussion to a specific genre. Let us suppose that you are a fan of science-fiction movies. You could explain the latest – or older- sci-fi movies to your audience. What is the story about? What does the ending mean? If a film was complicated (think Inception), then maybe you could simplify it for your audience.

Or you could talk about the latest entertainment updates, news, and titbits. Are you excited to about an upcoming TV show? What is the status of that new film project? Which actors are playing what roles?

You could even create videos of trailer reactions. You could show the trailer for a film or TV show and then give your feedback on it. Did it impress you? Did you notice any details in the trailer that you want to share? What are your thoughts on the casting choices?

There are many ways to approach this niche. The idea is to find out just exactly what interests you about a film or TV show. It could be the dialogues. If that is so, then you can talk about how dialogues impact different movies and TV shows. Maybe you are a fan of screenplays in films and TV. Or you could enjoy the atmosphere in a movie or TV show. Whatever your interests, you could talk in detail about the subject matter, using expert references and your own personal opinions.

YouTube Channels for Inspiration

- Screen Rant

- Lessons from the Screenplay

- Looper

- The Film Theorists

- Every Frame a Painting

Lists

Ever looked for "Top X Lists" on YouTube to see what the best options of a particular topic are?

When people want a quick rundown of a subject matter, they look to lists. Having a list-based channel is useful as you can keep the attention of the audience member for long. Their need to know the next entry on the list matches your intention to deliver an exciting menu.

One of the best features of a numbered list is that you do not have to appear on camera. Your voice is juxtaposed with clips of the subject you are talking about. However, if you are creating a "Top List" channel, then I recommend sticking to a particular topic. It could be movies, food, video games, fashion, or anything else. While you have the option to work with a number of subject matter, you should ideally pick one so that you can find your audience.

If you are asking why that is important, then let me put it this way. Let us say that you started out with a "Top 10 Videos Games of This Year" list. You suddenly find your channel flooded with viewers. You start gaining subscribers, who are eager to see the next content you have to post. Now let us assume that you decided to post a "Top 10 Fast Food Joints" list. You might leave your audience baffled and disappointed. They had returned to your channel because they expected you to talk about video games.

Once you find your subject, then you have a lot of content to work with.

If you are still apprehensive, then let me show you.

Let us say that you picked movies as your preferred topic. Here are some lists you can work with:

Top 10 Fantasy Movies of the Decade

Top 10 Actors Who Did Have Not Received an Oscar

Top 10 Sidekicks in Movie History

Top 10 Movies with The Best Visual Effects

I just came up with those topics on the fly. Imagine what you can accomplish when you are entirely focused on your channel and have the time to brainstorm ideas.

YouTube Channels for Inspiration

- WatchMojo

- Matthew Santoro - Matthew does not always post lists. But when he does, they are typically pure gold.

- MostAmazingTop10

- The Richest

News

People want to know about current affairs, whether locally or globally. But for many, flipping through TV channels to find the right source of news might be a daunting task.

Which brings us to a news channel on YouTube.

You could cover the news in two different ways.

You can appear on camera and give the audience a rundown of the news. You can combine that with your own opinions or merely state the facts as they are.

You can present the news in a voiceover format. This involves showing clips and images of the news topic and providing a running commentary in the background.

However, remember that if you are providing your views, your audience may not always welcome them. You might cover some sensitive news topics, and one wrong comment might encourage backlash from the public. If you are planning to provide your feedback in your news channel, I would recommend a neutral approach, free from any bias.

You can focus on local news topics and attract audiences from your own region or city. You could also focus on international news, approaching the niche from a broader perspective. Covering international news presents you with many topics. You might have to filter through these topics and choose those that you feel really matters to your audience. Talking about every news topic might take a long time.

While covering news, I believe that you should conduct heavy research into your topics. You might favor a specific newspaper or online publisher. But getting inputs from a variety of sources gives you the confidence to present your information. If you are covering international news, look through both global and local sources for facts and information.

YouTube Channels for Inspiration

- The Philip DeFranco Show

- Vox

- The Young Turks

- Nowthis

- Test Tube News

Tutorials

If you are experienced in a skill, then you could help others learn it as well.

You can approach this niche in plenty of ways, depending on the skill that you have.

If you are good at playing a musical instrument (or multiple instruments), then you could create tutorials for playing that instrument. You could start with the basics, move on to intermediate skills, and then show advanced techniques. You could give the audience some quick tips on handling the equipment and getting the right results.

But you do not have to create a tutorial channel for just music. Can you draw really well? Are you good at using editing software? How about acting or dancing classes? You could even focus on knitting, art, and singing as well. Makeup tutorials are somewhat popular on YouTube too.

While the above examples seek out a specific audience, you could try something for a general audience as well. DIY tutorials involve videos that many people can utilize in their everyday lives. If you feel that you have much to offer in the field, then you can go ahead make DIYs your channel's primary focus.

There are favorite channels on YouTube that even offer yoga tutorials.

Your skill is your market.

Focusing on this niche allows you to do what you are passionate about while gaining an audience for it and eventually, making money out of it.

A point to note is that your audience might judge your skills, which is inevitable as they approach your channel to learn something new. This does not mean that you should be concerned about your abilities. Instead, as you are giving tutorials to others, try to keep enhancing your experience as well. This will allow you to approach your channel with fresh ideas and even new concepts.

YouTube Channels for Inspiration

- Produce Like a Pro

- JamPlay

- Matt Steffanina

- Proko

- Chloe Morello

- Mad Stuff with Rob

Educational

Knowledge is power. And with a YouTube channel, you can be the one to spread that awareness and empower others.

Do you think you know a lot about a particular subject or are curious to find out more? Then you can turn your expertise and curiosity into a YouTube channel.

Say that you are a fan of Physics. You can create a channel that dives into numerous topics on the subject; you could also explain simple physics ideas. Furthermore, you could investigate more into theories and discoveries.

You could even combine physics and movies, where you talk about the physics of certain movie scenes. Was that stunt possible, could the missile fly in that manner, could Batman actually dodge that bullet, is The Matrix real? There is so much that you could talk about and it is only limited by your creativity.

Your videos can focus on any topic that you that interests you. It could be history, biology, chemistry, arts, literature, linguistics, and so much more.

You could approach this niche in two ways.

You could directly speak about the topic yourself.

Or you could create animations about the topic and then add in a voiceover.

When you start educating others, you could automatically establish yourself as an expert in the field. But I recommend staying abreast of new developments, information, and advancements (if any) if the field that you are focusing on. This gives you a lot more material to work with. So, do not hesitate to combine your area of study with other topics.

YouTube Channels for Inspiration

- Crash Course

- ASAP Science

- VSauce

- Kurzgesagt

- Veritasium

Automotive

Do you have access to vehicles? If so, then this could very well be the very thing your channel focuses on.

With the automotive section, you can talk about your favorite vehicles. You can show the vehicle's features, showcase its interiors and speak about its engine. You can take the car (or whatever sort of vehicle it happens to be) out for a test drive, grabbing beautiful shots of the ride in action.

Alternatively, your channel could be purely educational. You could talk about the various components in a vehicle, bring news about the automotive industry, check out new technology, and lots more.

If you choose to review vehicles, you might require a few pieces of advanced equipment. This is because you might need to take multiple shots simultaneously as you ride the car around.

Your channel does not always have to feature the most luxurious cars around. You could talk about vehicles commonly found in the market. You could even have a bit of fun with your channel, like the way they do it in Top Gear (which is one of the inspirations given below).

YouTube Channels for Inspiration

- RegularCars

- Motor Trend Channel

- Top Gear

- ChrixFix

With that, I have given you a few ideas to work with. But remember that this list is not a comprehensive list of topics that you can work on. Your channel could be on celebrity gossip, pranks, comics, sports, parodies, and a lot more.

Think of a niche as an opportunity to use your expertise, skills, or experience to create content. Most importantly, it allows you to have a lot of fun.

How Often is Too Often?

Last Week Tonight is a popular news and satirical channel on YouTube. They churn out content once every week on Mondays.

But other channels post on a much more frequent basis. So why is there a disparity between any two given channels on YouTube? Is there a specific number of times to publish that could get you better results?

Before I answer that question. Let me ask you this; are you able to keep your audiences watching your videos? How early do they drop off from your video? How many viewers watch your entire video? What is the average time your audience spends on your videos?

The reason I propose the above questions is that if you cannot get your audience to watch your content, then the frequency of your uploads will not give you better results. You could post five times a day. But if your videos do not garner interest, then all the effort you place into creating those five videos just goes to waste.

To find out more about your videos, you need to use analytics.

YouTube gives you detailed insights into your videos, so make use of those insights to gain in-depth information about your content. To go to YouTube analytics, just click on your profile icon and then follow the below steps:

Click on the "Creator Studio" option in the drop-down menu

Next, in the options tab where you can see links such as "Dashboard" and "Video Manager," look for a section named "Analytics." Click on it.

Once you reach your Analytics page, look for a tab named "Audience retention" and click on that.

You will notice two sections, "Average View Duration" and "Average Percentage Viewed." If these two sections show low results, then you should perform a detailed study of your videos.

What do I mean by low results?

Let us assume that you upload videos that are 10 minutes long. If you have an Average View Duration of 5 minutes, then that means that your audience watch at least 50% of your video. That is not so bad because you should always expect people to drop off your video.

Drop-offs could happen for many reasons:

- The viewer might have to leave the computer or device to perform some other task

- Poor network connectivity

- Viewers are satisfied with the content they received so far

- The audience is not interested in your videos

However, whatever the reason, video drop-offs exist in all videos so you can never really get a 100% Average View Duration.

However, reaching 50% is a good average when you are starting out.

Let us assume that your Average View Duration is only four minutes. This means that you get roughly 40% average percentage of views.

That is a cause for concern.

Now, why do videos have drop-off points? Well, the next time you analyze your video, find out where you have these mass drop-offs. In other words, at what point in your video do you have people exit in large numbers. Head back to your video and find out what happens at that point in the video.

Perhaps you might be talking too much at that point. There could be a long music sequence that is boring for your audience. You could also have animations that are uncomfortable to watch. Moreover, there could be any number of things.

Make a note of them.

Then watch other videos that you have uploaded and then start making notes on those videos. Over time, you might notice patterns that show you why exactly your audience is leaving your videos at certain times.

The fact that something is repeatedly happening and is causing your audience to leave should convince you to change it.

When you have drop-offs, changing your schedule does not boost the numbers or improve your statistic.

Another factor that you should pay attention to is the clicks.

You should find out if your thumbnails and your titles are generating clicks to your video. This is essential for two reasons:

- You find out if you have enough traffic combing over to your channel. Without visitors to your video, you will not be able to get the right audience. They are being stopped by the fact that your thumbnails and titles are not interesting enough.

- Your clicks affect your traffic in another way, and it has got to do with YouTube. When you receive low clicks, then YouTube might demote your videos. In this way, your videos will begin to fall down in rankings every time someone searches YouTube using a query related to your video. Likewise, if you generate better clicks, YouTube will promote your video and suggest it to a broader audience automatically.

Let me explain this with an example.

Let us say that your video is about discovering street food in Turkey. So ideally, your video should appear if a user enters any one of the below terms:

- Street food

- Turkey

- Explore

- Middle Eastern cuisine

Let us say that your video used to perform consistently around the ninth spot when people searched YouTube using the query "Street food."

If you do not start generating clicks to your content, you will find other videos that have better clicks overtaking your content. That means that you might eventually notice your video falling down to the eleventh position, then moving further down to the nineteenth position and so on.

Because many users are churning out content, YouTube gives priority to those videos that are roping in clicks and views.

Which is why, when you notice poor numbers, you need to go through the rest of your Analytics section as well. This part of YouTube will be your best guide in understanding the engagement, interest, reach, and views that your videos receive. With these metrics – and a lot more – you can start working on improving your content. As you make adjustments, you may notice a change in the statistics. People will respond to the improvements you make and your videos will garner better attention and, more importantly, longer retention.

When you have reached a good retention level based on the timing of your videos, and received better clicks, then you can move on to your schedule.

Figuring out the right schedule for your channel depends on a few factors:

Is YouTube Your Full Time Gig?

If your answer to the question is yes, then you should seriously consider uploading content more frequently than others. However, consider the next question before setting an uploading schedule in stone.

How Much Time Do You Need To Make a YouTube Video?

If you can create a video in under six hours, then maybe you could think about releasing four or more videos a week. Do give yourself a couple of days break. This is not just to take some time off and allow yourself to research more ideas. But you can use this time to jump back to Analytics. Check out the progress of your videos. Find out where you should make improvements. Keep making your videos better.

If you have decided that you are still going to create more videos per week, then it is time to move on to the next question.

Can You Produce Content Regularly?

If you are capable of launching up to five videos per week, then that is spectacular. However, do you have enough content to create such a schedule? Do not imagine the near present. Think of the future. Can you continue to generate content to publish five videos a week?

CrashCourse is an interesting channel that focuses on taking complex ideas and creating short and simple versions of them in order to make it easy for viewers to consume the video content. They create three videos per week, but still have over 10 million subscribers. What is the secret to their content? That depends on the next point.

Can You Keep Your Content Interesting?

The frequency of content is not the only factor that comes into play here. You have to be sure that the content you create will have consistent levels of engagement, interest, and information. It is one thing to create a frequent schedule. It is yet another to maintain high-quality content throughout your timeline.

What If You Cannot Create Content Frequently?

If you are going to spend time on YouTube to focus on creating content and generate income from it, you might need to devote a large portion of your time on the platform. It is true that the quality of your content matters. Some channels create just two videos per week and receive a nice substantial amount of engagements. However, the frequency is the key here as you do not want your audience to forget about your channel.

How frequently you can create videos is entirely up to you. Know that when your audience become interested in your videos, they seek out more of them. If you are building a brand on YouTube, then you need to meet the demands of your audience as much as possible.

By that, you do not have to upload every day. However, think about pushing out at least two videos per week.

If you do cannot create content frequently, then you should consider taking the time to generate genuinely engaging content. While you might not achieve the same level of progress when you upload videos regularly, you will still be able to attract an audience for your videos.

Another thing to note is that every video you upload is a step forward to achieving your goals. Furthermore, each time you upload a video, you get more data to use. That said, more data leads to improvement and that in turn may well yield better content.

Additionally, more videos retain your channel's impression in the minds of your audience. They easily recollect your videos because they have seen it often.

Here is something that I would like to point out. You need to keep a good work and life balance. Burnouts are possible when working on YouTube so remember that pushing yourself too much just to upload content does not give you any benefit.

The most important rule of content is; quantity over quality.

Timing is Crucial

To decide on the right time for posting your content can be tricky. There are no set rules or guidelines to determine when your videos could gain the best views. You might be lucky on a particular day, or your videos could perform at an average pace on that same day.

What truly matters is the content. This is because once people enjoy your content and watch more of your videos, your channel starts appearing under the "Recommended" section of their YouTube main page. Additionally, your content will also begin to show up as automatic suggestions once someone completes watching a particular video.

However, this does not mean that no study has been committed to discovering the ideal times to post your videos.

According to a study conducted by Frederator, a multi-channel network based in New York, you should post your videos during the below timings to get the most – or fastest - views:

- Between 2 PM to 4 PM from Mondays to Wednesdays

- Between 12 PM to 3 PM on Thursdays and Fridays

- Between 9 AM to 11 AM on Saturdays and Sundays

Do note that the above recommendations are based on Eastern Standard Time. Additionally, if you are in one of the countries that have Fridays and Saturdays, or Thursdays and Fridays as their designated weekends, then perhaps you could use the recommendation for Saturdays and Sundays (where you post between 9 AM to 11 AM local time).

You can post content during any month of the year. However, May and September are the worst months to publish your video. This is because these months are when people take vacations, schools and universities either complete or start terms, sporting seasons begin or people generally get involved in outdoor activities.

These are pretty good timings to start off with when you have just launched your channel.

However, when you begin to upload more videos, you need to rely on Analytics to find out when is the best time to upload videos.

Head back over to your channel's analytics section. Click on the tab that says "Realtime." Here you can notice the numbers of view you get across 48 hours, shown under the title "Last 48 hours". The views are displayed as a chart. This means that you will notice highs and lows spread across the table. You take the time when you have the highest views and upload your video just a short period before the chart starts showing the rise.

As the chart shows the views across 48 hours, I would recommend recording the views over a week or even two weeks. If the views consistently appear during a specific period, then you know when the right time to upload your next videos is.

Put More Emphasis on Videos That Are Working For You

As the years go by, more and more content creators are entering YouTube's virtual space. This means that while you have the opportunity to build your brand properly, you won't get a lot of opportunities to test out different kinds of content. Here is what you should be doing instead:

Double down on the content that works for you. Keep churning out the videos that your community loves to watch. If you would like to try out an innovative idea, then inform your community that you would like to do so. Once you have informed them, you can actually involve them in the content creation process. You might get some valuable feedback from them that you can use to improve your content.

Make Full Use of The Discussion Forums

YouTube has now given you the power to hold discussions with your community. Ask them a question, keep them updated about new stuff, or get them excited for a new video.

Do you want to get their opinion on a piece of content? You can hold polls where you can include options for your community to select, or they can add their own options.

Some YouTubers also actively engage their audience through the discussion forums. When they delay publishing a video because of certain personal or other issues, they inform their community. You will be surprised at the amount of support you can get from people around the world who enjoy your content.

You can also ask your community what kind of content they would like to see next. You can either give them options or if your community knows the type of content you create, allow them to freely give you options.

You can even have a casual conversation with them. But do note that if too many updates from you are unimportant and merely casual talk, then your audience might stop depending on your updates for any valuable information. That's a surefire way to alienate your audience.

Understand How Google AI Works

Remember that Google's AI can not only listen to sounds, but can also recognize images and patterns. This means that you should be extra careful about using someone else's content, as that can be identified by the platform and flagged as a copyright breach.

New Content

YouTube has changed its algorithm slightly. New videos automatically get ranked high. YouTube has taken this step in order to encourage creators to produce more content on their channel. The more videos you create, the more chances you have of gaining an audience.

Let's look at an example to highlight this point. Imagine that you have created a new video on Sunday. The video is automatically ranked high, which means that you are more likely to target a larger audience. Let's say that your next video comes out on Wednesday, you once again gain access to a large volume of views and interactions. As you consistently create content, you are going to consistently keep targeting a large volume of viewers quickly. Let's say that you create one video per week. Once you gain a large audience for one video, the ranking of your video will go down in order to give space for other creators on the platform. Because you are not creating a video quickly enough, you are not creating constant content to keep your channel on a high level of rating. And that eventually might affect the number of video views.

But remember that consistent video uploads isn't the only thing that you should be focusing on. Quality matters!

Think of it this way. Imagine that you create high-quality content and you receive a lot of views on the video. The high views automatically boost the videos ratings. Why?

Let's look at YouTube's main goals. Like any website, YouTube values the time people spend on the platform. The more time and more traffic the website receives, the stronger its position in the global internet traffic share. Guess how it gets to accomplish that?

That's right. The traffic that it receives on its videos; the same videos that are created by you and every other content creator. For that reason, YouTube's algorithm automatically rewards people who bring more traffic to the website.

Positive Interactions Are Rewarded

Those likes and shares? They are not just for show. They add value to your channel. Have you noticed how content creators ask their audience to leave a like or comment and subscribe to the channel? Each positive interaction helps boost the engagement of the video. The more likes and comments you collect, the better ranking the video receives.

YouTube rewards high engagement by recommending your videos to more people. They might start noticing your video on their main feed or on the right-hand column of a video.

Chapter 3:
The Importance of Quality Content

As I mentioned earlier in the book, YouTube success is not solely about the quantity of your content. You can generate a tremendous amount of material in a single week. That said, if you don't have an audience built up for your videos, then you might notice that finding traction on YouTube is an uphill battle.

Which is why I want to place a particular emphasis on generating quality content. I will help you to polish your videos and give you useful tips to capture your videos.

But first, a little bit having authority. And by that, I do not mean being in command.

The Psychology of Authority

There is a term name Authoritative Marketing. Basically, this means you essentially use your knowledge in a particular field and establish yourself as an expert in that field. You develop an "authority" status in your area of focus. By building this level of influence, you get to reach out to a broader audience network and can even convert your viewers to customers.

That sounds like something you are probably going to achieve from YouTube anyway right? So why be an authority?

I'll shed some light on this particular issue below.

Customers or Clients will Come to You

You must have seen YouTube channels collaborate with brands and companies. You might think that once you start generating content, then this might happen to you quickly. The reality is slightly more complicated; brands trust someone who can represent them well. Meaning, that most brands want to be associated with a YouTube personality consisting of experience and knowledge in his or her field. Sephora approaches beauty vloggers who have impressive skills. Mercedes-Benz will only look to work with those video vloggers who have excellent command over their automotive content. This works for every single field.

When you set yourself up as an authority in your field, you automatically begin to attract the attention of big brands and businesses. They in turn would like you to promote their products or services.

Similarly, customers trust you and your content. When you begin to sell your products, merchandise, or services, your audience will be eager to get them. This is because being authoritative in your content has given you a level of respect from your audience. They do not mind supporting your channel and your business.

Save Money on Advertising

When you start making waves as someone knowledgeable about your content, then people start referring you to others. This, in turn, creates a powerful word-of-mouth marketing structure for you. Eventually, when you are ready to reach out to businesses or brands to endorse your channel, launch your product, or market yourself more, you might have an easier time getting them on board your plans.

Building a Network

You might have noticed that often, big YouTube names appear on other YouTube channels. Or some channels receive special celebrity guest stars. This occurs when people realize that you are well-versed in the content you are providing them. If you have an educational channel that is producing some excellent content, you can easily find NASA assisting you with some of your videos. If you have been showing some incredible skills in cooking, you could feature yourself on the Tasty network and spread your fame.

Opening New Doors

Your YouTube channel will only be one source of revenue. Events, collaborations, product lines, network deals, and more are just a few other options that become available to you. As you develop your authority further, you gain opportunities to become part of events, interviews, and more. These open up more doors for you, where you can find better means to market yourself, create a product, start a business or brand, and more.

Good Mythical Morning is a comedy show on YouTube. Now, you might think that someone who focuses on the comedy niche might not have much authority in the field. After all, it is not like educational content where you can show how smart and informed you are.

You might just be mistaken there.

There are many ways to show authority in your field. You can demonstrate your expertise through knowledge of the area. Or you can create content that shows how experienced you are in what you do.

The creators of Good Mythical Morning, Rhett McLaughlin and

Link Neal, have created so much high-quality content that they have been featured on talk shows, had celebrities appear on their channel, and even got acquired by another favorite channel; Smosh.

The point is, you have to show that you are good at creating quality content. Your channel's videos should be consistent, innovative, and never lose the personality you imbue within them. Of course, you might not have much authority to show when you begin working on your channel. But by maintaining quality content, it won't be long before you are having celebrities appearing in your videos or appearing in talk-shows or getting requests for acquisitions.

Being Part of Big Events

Seán William McLoughlin, also popularly known as Jacksepticeye, has now hosted game award shows. Markiplier has his own interactive series.

When you start creating quality content, you automatically start making waves in various parts of the media and entertainment industry. Some YouTubers have gone on to act in movies while others have written their own books. YouTube opens up a whole new world of opportunities for you once you tap into its potential.

Pretty soon, you can fund your own content and spread word of it to other people. What do I mean by funding your own content? For example, you could have an animated series created about you, publish your own book series, and more!

Creating Quality Content

So we have reached the part where you know how to understand your analytics. You are ready to create your first batch of videos.

Now you are wondering what exactly constitutes a "high-quality" video.

When someone mentions quality, people immediately think about expensive equipment, impressive visual effects in their videos, and probably having a good set.

On the contrary, many YouTube channels push out great content using their mobile devices. They do not invest in acquiring more tools unless it is necessary to do so.

So how can one create quality content? Here are a few steps that might get you inspired.

Develop Consistency

I have placed emphasis on this point several times, and I will do so again. Before we dive into actually creating the content, you must decide to keep a regular timetable. You could have a degree in moviemaking, but if it takes you three months to create and upload your videos to YouTube, you probably won't be able to keep the attention of your audience for long. They may not want to wait for more content to come.

The first thing you should focus on is streamlining your video creation process. If you can get more people involved to work on your video, that is great. Otherwise, create an editing template that will help you quickly edit your videos and upload them. If you are not experienced in developing video templates, then you could seek out someone who can help you with it.

Look online for freelancers who might be able to assist you with making an editing template for you.

You could do it on your own by merely heading directly over to

YouTube itself and looking at some great tutorials.

You can also set up a studio at your home. This does not have to be a costly endeavor. You can buy most of the items you require for a relatively affordable price.

You Need to 'Hook' Your Viewers

There are many ways to develop a hook, depending on the content you are creating.

If you have a DIY channel, you could start by showing the result at first and then slowly taking the audience through the steps to reach that result.

If you have a travel blog, you can run through some beautiful shots of the location you are going to cover. Then you could start your video going into details of your travel destination.

For videos where you cannot show the results start with a story, a question, or even an interesting welcome note. Look at any HD video from The Philip DeFranco Show, and you will see how the introduction merely is unique and works well for the channel.

VSauce is another channel that begins their videos with intriguing questions and engaging stories. When you start watching their videos, you just have this urge to know more about the content.

Find your hook. Take inspiration from those who have already done it before and discover what works for you.

Short Opening Credits

Look to KinoCheck, a channel that focuses on showing the latest movie trailers, entertainment highlights, and news. They feature a short title sequence that is unique to their channel. It is no longer than five seconds, which means it does not destroy the flow of the video.

Whether you choose to make your opening sequence quirky, serious, or educational, you need to check your drop-offs. If viewers are dropping off during the title sequence, then you might need to change it to something else or keep it shorter.

End Screens

When your video ends, you have the opportunity to take your audience to your other videos. You can do this by adding a unique graphic that provides a link to videos, channels, or even websites. Note that you can only add end screens to the last 20 seconds of your video.

To add your end screens, just follow the below steps:

- Click on your profile icon and then click on Creator Studio.

- On the list of tabs that you can see, head over to the Video Manager tab

- Choose the video that you would like to add an end screen to and click the "Edit" button found right below the video

- Next, select the option "End Screen & Annotations"

- At the next screen, you will be able to add up to four buttons to your end screen. These are:

  - Video or playlist: This option takes your viewers to another video or the playlist of your channel.

  - Channel: You can use this option to promote other

channels. These could be your own channels or someone else's, if you are collaborating with them.

- Subscribe: This button is a graphical subscribe display that gets overlaid on your video. You can use this button to increase the chances of new potential audience members subscribing to your video.

- Link: You can place links to your website so you can drive traffic to another source through your videos.

- To add these buttons, just click on the "Add element" option and in the drop-down menu that follows and add your preferred button by selecting "Create".

- If you would like to check the preview of your end screen, simply click the "Preview" button.

- When you are confident about the way your end screen looks, just click "Save" and you are done!

You can create the end screen in several unique ways.

One of the options you can use is to arrange the buttons in such a manner that there is space for you to appear in the video. You can then start engaging with your audience and encourage them to click on each option. You could even give a brief explanation to where each button will take the viewer. Remember, you have 20 seconds to make sure you keep it concise and straight-to-the-point. Also remember to show enthusiasm when you are promoting videos, channels, polls or links. This shows your audience that you are eager to show them more content and might increase the chances of click-throughs.

Here are a few things you should remember when working with the "End screen & Annotations" tab.

- You can use either the End screen feature or the Annotations feature. You cannot place both into your video.

- If you chose to add a Video or Playlist, then you get three options. These options are listed below:

  - Most recent upload: When you use this option, you automatically get to add your most recently uploaded video to your end screen.

  - Best for viewer: With this option, you let YouTube select and add a video to the end screen. YouTube will pick a video from your channel that that best suits the viewer.

  - Choose a video or a playlist: Using this option, you will be able to select what video or playlist you would like to feature on the end screen.

- When you choose each element, a shape appears on your video. You can adjust the position of the shape and even increase or decrease its size, depending on how you would like to place it. Work around this feature to see what style fits your video or how you would like to approach your end screen.

- Remember that you can use the End Screen option on the last 20 seconds of your video. Try to create your videos by keeping that factor in mind.

- As mentioned before, you can add up to four elements to your video. However, one of the parts has to be a video or a playlist. You could even add multiple videos to your end screen. With that in mind, you can add a video by choosing the "Best for viewer" option and another one using either the "Most recent upload" option or the "Choose a video or a playlist" selection. This gives you many ways to bring exposure to your channel and your content.

- We are now going back to Analytics. Yes, that magical domain that will be your best friend to discover insights and improve your video a lot more. Click on your profile icon, select Creator Studio, and head over to the Analytics tab. In the screen that presents itself, choose the "End screen element" option. In this section, you will be able to see how your end screens are performing. This is a powerful way to work with your elements and change them accordingly.

Edit Silences or Distractions

The trick to creating good content is to know how and what to edit from your video. By this, I do not mean that you need to get yourself a year's experience in editing. What I mean is that you should find those parts of the video that do not have to be there and crop them out. And doing that does not require professional editing skills.

Let me explain this to you in another way. Have you ever watched a YouTube video that involves a person speaking to the camera? If you have, you might notice that the entire video is divided into many segments. You might see multiple cuts, where the person is speaking about something, and then when he or she completes that part, the video immediately cuts to the next segment. It happens so subtly that we do not pay attention to it. This method is called "jump cuts". This is what you should focus on as well.

Not everyone has the latent abilities of Steven Spielberg or David Fincher. But you can edit your videos to make them look like they were created by a professional. There is a simple way to do this.

Record your video however you can. You do not have to be perfect in the way you record. Create multiple versions of your video, if you are able to. Do not worry if you end up fumbling when creating your content or making inevitable mistakes. Ignore the fact that you have long pauses in your video.

When you finish recording, bring your clips together in a coherent manner. Remove the pauses and long stretches of content. Take out the parts that do not add value to your video. Bring together those parts that you feel fit together well.

Of course, you might find that you may not do it well the first time around. That is okay. Editing is a learning process. With each edit, you understand how to do it better. You can even use the help of Analytics to understand what part of your content you should edit and what you can keep.

Lights, Camera, and Studio!

Now that we have covered some tips on creating quality content, we will put some focus on the more technical aspects of your video.

Let us go right ahead and dive into the camera section.

Getting the Right Camera

You are going to spend a lot of time in front of your camera, so let us discuss some good camera options.

You could either spend on an inexpensive model or, if you have the resources, get yourself an expensive tool. I could also recommend some of the latest smartphones in the market. They come equipped with a good quality camera to record your videos. Some even have specific editing functionalities should you be interested.

Inexpensive Options

When you are short on budget, or you only want to buy a cheap camera for a test run, you can look to Logitech for help. I recommend the Logitech C299 or the C270 for this purpose. The camera allows you to record in HD quality and you can attach it to your computer using a USB cable. However, the USB cable might also be the camera's shortcoming, as you will not be able to take it with you. You could of course, carry your laptop around with you with the camera connected to it, but I might not recommend it when shooting videos for the travel and restaurant review category.

Getting a portable camera might require a little more investment, but the one that I found which has good quality and is relatively cheap is the Canon PowerShot ELPH.

For a Bigger Budget

If you have the budget to spare for an expensive camera, then consider the Canon EOS 5D Mark IV camera. The price point is high, but you get to shoot in spectacular 4K quality. A slightly less pricey option would be the Canon EOS 80D or the Nikon D5300.

Important Notes

- When you are recording yourself, look at the camera. This ensures that you are looking at the audience in the final cut of your video.

- Hold the camera in the landscape orientation and not the portrait. This is so that they get a broader angle, even if means focusing on yourself, particularly your upper body.

- Position the camera so that it is arranged slightly above eye level. Do not keep it too high or it will be uncomfortable for you, and it is not a spectacular angle for your viewers. Do not keep it too low either as people might get a view of your chin. Don't worry, there is nothing wrong with your chin. When talking into a camera, looking straight at it shows confidence and gives the audience a better view of your face.

- Make use of platforms such as Dropbox to transfer files from one place to another if required.

- Always make sure you have sufficient memory, whether using your smartphone or a camera. If you are using a camera, make sure that you have additional memory cards with you.

Stabilizing the View

We talked about placing your device at the ideal spot. But how can one keep a device at that spot for an extended period?

It is simple; you get yourself a tripod.

If you do not want to spend on getting a separate tripod, you could use a stack of books, a box, or another surface to position your camera. You might not get the ideal angle, but it might do the trick for specific devices. This technique works well with mobile devices, as they are light and easy to position.

Inexpensive Options

There are a few budget-friendly options in the market. If I had to combine both quality and price, I would recommend the Manfrotto PIXI Evo 2 tripod or the slightly pricier Compact Tripod from Nikon. The Manfrotto is an especially great start for vloggers who might travel a lot for their videos.

Do note that these tripods are best suited for lightweight devices. I would not recommend placing a DSLR on them.

For a Bigger Budget

Joby Gorillapod SLR is an incredible tripod to use. One of the best features of the tripod is its versatility, making it ideal for almost any vlogging idea. Want to shoot at home? Sure, you can do that. Will you be traveling a lot? You can take this tripod with you. Its versatility comes from the fact that its legs are flexible, instead of the typical rigid legs you find in most tripods. This allows you to attach it to practically any surface.

Another tripod that you can consider is the Magnus VT-4000, which allows you to mount many cameras, even the slightly heavier ones.

Lighting

Great lighting equipment not only illuminates your face correctly, but it is essential when you are editing the video as well. Poor lighting tends to keep your audience away from your videos and even create an awkward atmosphere.

If you are not planning on spending on lighting equipment, then you can rely on the big ball of fire in the sky. Yes, I am talking about the sun.

Natural lighting is perfect for most settings. Try and find a spot or an area where there is sufficient sunlight. Make sure you are facing the sun so that your face is shown clearly. If you have the sunlight behind you, your face might appear in silhouette.

You could also make use of a desk lamp or your room's lighting for additional light.

Inexpensive Options

For some budget-friendly options for lighting, I would recommend the Neewer CN 16 LED light. It does not have all the features that you find with a piece of professional lighting equipment, but it helps illuminate your face properly. The Neewer is also ideal for travel, making it easier to take it with you to other locations.

Another option would be the Cowboy Studio Triple Lighting Kit. This equipment comes with two white umbrellas, three 45-watt bulbs, three stands, and a carry case. While you can take this kit along with you during your travels, you might not find it ideal to use in any location. However, for your home or studio, this makes for a beautiful lighting companion.

For a Bigger Budget

If you can shell out some cash for more equipment, then you might have to consider getting multiple tools. One of the best pieces of lighting equipment is the Aputure Amaran AL-528S. What makes this lighting gear so ideal is that it features LED lights that you can mount on a stand. You might also consider getting a couple of reflectors. Ideally, you could use the Neewer Multi-Light Reflector for this purpose.

Speak Up!

Now that we have covered the visual part of your video let us jump into the audio. When you are recording your video, it is imperative that your audience can hear you clearly. No one will try to strain his or her attention figuring out what you are trying to say. Additionally, remember that hook I had mentioned earlier? The one that could help you grab your audience's attention instantly? Well, if you want to make that happen, you might also require a good quality microphone.

Worry not, I have a few recommendations for you.

For those of you who are just starting out or would like to stick to a budget-friendly option, then you could go for the Samson Portable Mic or eBerry Cobblestone Microphone. Both these options provide good quality results, and you can easily carry them around with you.

If you are using smartphones to record video, then perhaps you could also consider choosing a lavalier microphone. You might have seen them used in stage plays, in presentations or on TV; they are mics that you can clip to your shirt or a surface for hands-free speaking capability.

The Seacue 3.5mm Lavalier mic is a convenient piece of tech to have. You merely have to plug the 3.5mm jack into your phone and you are done. This mic is excellent for videos where you have to travel or move around a lot. For a slightly higher price, you can get a lavalier mic with a few additional features. The PowerDeWise Professional is one such option for you. One of the best features of this mic is that it is useful in suppressing the noise of the wind. This is something you might find helpful for outdoor videos.

If you are willing to spend even more, here are a few options that might interest you. I would recommend USB microphones such as the Rode NT-USB or the Blue Yeti, the latter being quite popular among YouTubers. You could also use XLR microphones such as the AT2035 by Audio-Technica (though you might require a boom arm) or the Procaster by Rode.

Background Check

Having a nice background adds quality to your videos. In fact, they can set the tone for your content. I will discuss the atmosphere later in this chapter, but for now, let us work on giving your video a bit more personality.

If you do not want to invest in a background, then you can use what you have at home. Ideally, having a bookcase is a cool addition. You could also show your comic book, action figures, or makeup collections if your video is focused on such themes. Travelers can use a wall with a large map. Food vloggers can shoot their videos in their kitchen. In such small ways, you could find a background in your home. You could also potted plants in your background environment. Well, that said, the potted plants might cost a bit extra though.

For a small budget, you can get a decent background for yourself. First, think about getting a backdrop stand for yourself. The LimoStudio AGG112 Backdrop Stand could be a good option for you. Once you have the stand, then you can work on your backdrop itself. The PRO Photo Studio background options from Neewer are inexpensive.

For a bigger budget, you could find a whole lot of options that feature designs and patterns. These could be ideal for certain types of categories like fashion, beauty, art and so on.

A note that I would like to mention here is that you should choose backgrounds based on your content. For example, if your channel focuses beauty, then choose muted colors because the focus should be on your face.

However, if your videos are comedic, then bright colors definitely help set the mood. Your audience will immediately react to your background and might unconsciously prepare themselves for something colorful, fun, and quirky.

Jumping the Line

Your audience needs to remain interested in your video. Talk about something for too long, and your viewers will quickly exit your channel. Keep a pause for too long, and they are already clicking on the next video to watch, and it might not be yours.

So how can you keep your content fresh, even though it might exceed ten or maybe even twenty minutes?

Well, you use jump cuts.

Remember when I mentioned earlier about using specific cuts to remove long pauses, repetitive content or even unnecessary parts? Well, here, I will show you how to do those cuts.

So first things first, let us boot up your editing software. If you are currently scratching your head wondering, "what the heck does this person mean by editing software?", Then I will discuss more on that in the next segment. For now, let us work on trying to find out how to create jump cuts.

In your editing software, you might have a collection of videos that you might put together. The best way to create a jump cut is to work on each clip. It makes your task easier. Also, when you put all your edited clips together, you will be ready with the final video. If not, you might find yourself editing the entire video, which could take you a long while.

Whenever you are ready, go ahead and refer to the below steps:

- Select the video clip that you want to work on.

- Now play the video clip and note down all the parts that you want to remove. You should be able to note down the exact times to start and end the cut. Pause the video if you like every time you make a note to make the process easier for you. You could also work on the video frame by frame to make accurate cuts.

- For example, let us say that your video clip has a long pause from the ten-second mark until the fourteen-second mark. You should make a note that your cut should begin at the ten-second mark and end at the fourteen-second mark. By going through that part frame-by-frame, you can narrow down the exact moment when the silence starts.

- Once you have made a note of all the sections you want to be removed, use the cut tool (typically appearing as a scissor icon) or use a specific button (some software allow you to use the delete button) to cut off those sections.

- Go through the other clips and repeat Step two and Step three.

When you are ready, you can put your clips together.

The Right Software

There are tons of editing software that you can use for your YouTube videos. I have broken down the best software into three segments; free (who does not like some free stuff?), budget-friendly, and expensive.

Let us begin with those you do not have to pay to get.

Free

If you are using a Windows platform, then you should already have the Windows Movie Maker software. If not, you can always get it for free. Movie Maker is easy to use and provides quite a few selections of transitions that you can use if you are interested in doing so. However, it has limited editing tools that you can use. It is perfect for beginners who do not want to spend a lot of time editing their videos.

For Mac users, you should have iMovie installed on your computer. It provides useful tools to help you work on your videos, but like the Windows Movie Maker, it does feature many editing options. One of the notable features of iMovie is that you can fix certain shaky cam movements. This is ideal if you move with your camera a lot.

Another software that you can get for free is Blender. One of the cool features of this software is that you can work with 3D graphics. While there are limited 3D options to choose from, it is an excellent addition that gives you a fair amount of flexibility.

Budget-Friendly Software

With a little budget to spend, you could invest in a decent software that could cater to all your editing requirements. I will list a few that I would recommend, though the market has many options for you.

Pinnacle Studio 20 is a software that gives you many features at an affordable price point. It is easy to use and provides you with multi-camera editing. You have enough effects to add to your content to make it more than unique. Moreover, you can upload your videos directly to your YouTube channel as soon as you are done.

Sony Movie Studio Platinum is another inexpensive option. A standout feature of this software is its incredible rendering speed, making it ideal for you to get your video ready quicker. You can also directly upload your video to YouTube. It features a collection of transition effects suitable for beginners.

If you can add a little more to your budget, you could choose Adobe Premiere Elements 11. The software is user-friendly, features a ton of effects, and includes some incredible, excellent features taken from another of Adobe's products; the bestselling Adobe Premiere Pro.

Expensive

Finally, we come to those products that might involve a sizeable investment from you, but they pack a whole lot of features and capabilities.

I am going to recommend two products; one for Mac and one for Windows. I find these products ideal for everyone, from beginners to professionals.

The first one is the Final Cut Pro X, the software features a friendly user-interface. You can get started on it with relative ease. It includes enough features to turn your video into a professional masterpiece. It gives you a speedy performance, involves plenty of effects, and packs in great editing tools.

For Windows, I recommend Vegas Pro. The software is pretty heavy-duty, so you might need to have a laptop that can handle its capabilities. However, you get numerous features and tools for editing, including the multi-cam editing feature. The Vegas pro is seriously robust software that you might need to get used to first.

Filming Your Video

Many elements go into filing your video. It is not as easy as deciding that you will have a close-up of your face and hit the record button. You need to develop your own style for making videos that will reflect in the final video as well. Which is why I thought it would be beneficial if you understood how to create a fantastic atmosphere in your video.

Get Your Style Ready

So the first factor that you should focus on is getting your style in place. Your style refers to the way you will be recording all your videos. In essence, it is the personality of your content.

To set up your style, here are a few points you should examine.

Location or Setting: Will you be recording your video outside or inside? Will it be inside your room, office, garage or kitchen? Each of these settings sends a story across toy our viewer.

Clothing: Your clothing is a reflection of your content as well. If you are dressed in formal wear, it probably indicates that you are going to talk about a serious topic. Semi-formal wear might be ideal for educational videos, where you are showing that you are knowledgeable, but not going to make your videos too serious. Think about your content and choose your attire accordingly.

Props: You do not require accessories for every form of video. However, it does add a level of quirkiness and fun, ideal for videos that focus on beauty, fashion, and technology to name a few.

Backdrop: I discussed this earlier, and your background makes a lot of difference in your video. Your office setting could be a background. Your garden might be used as a background for fitness videos. If you have a great view outside your window, you could use that as well.

Music: Music sets the tone effectively. It creates an atmosphere that reflects the theme of your videos. Have a piece of slow-paced suspense music gives the audience a different message than Chopin's compositions. You should also focus on the volume of the music. If it is too loud, it might be a distraction and cause discomfort to the audience. If it is too low, then its effects are lost.

Sound Effects: Similar to props, you do not need sound effects for your videos, but they do indeed add a little uniqueness to your content. If you are creating funny, videos, you might use sounds effects like crickets chirping and wolves howling to add a bit of fun.

While your style is entirely up to you, ensure that you keep it consistent between all your videos. This allows you to establish an identity that your audience will remember when the next time they enter YouTube.

Frame Your Video

A frame is a window to your video. It shows your audience information about you through your content.

Your frame should contain the vital information necessary for your content.

Depending on your content, you will choose the view that is ideal for the audience. For example, if you are a cooking-based channel, you will keep most of the video focus on the food. If you focus the camera on yourself, you might include the view of your kitchen.

The frame you choose depends on the shot. There are three main types of shots you can work with for your YouTube video.

Wide Shot

This shot is useful to show a lot of content or if you have many people in the video. Travel bloggers might use this shot a lot. If you are your friend decide to create videos together, then you might use this shot quite often. Automotive channels are another example who might find wide angled shots useful for their content.

Medium Shot

The medium shot puts you in focus, but also includes a little bit of the background. Remember when I discussed the background early and mentioned something about bookcases? Well, with a medium angled shot, you will be the focus, but the audience can see the bookshelf behind you as well.

Close Up Shot

This type of shot is all about you. You will cover most of the frame, as you are the one delivering the content. Beauty vloggers use this shot, as do numerous educational channels.

Important Notes

The rule "one size fits all" does not apply here. You may be able to work with just one frame for your videos. Or you might have to switch between frames to get the best angles. For example, travel vloggers often use close-ups or medium shots when they are directly talking to the camera. When they switch to their surroundings or the scenery, they prefer to use wide angled shots to get as much of the scene as possible.

Let us take another example. If you have a cooking channel, then you might use medium shots when you are talking to the camera. When the focus on the content shifts to the food and the method of cooking, then you might adopt a close-up shot. Closing in on the food allows you to let the audience see the results of your steps.

My recommendation is to experiment with your content and see what fits your YouTube niche.

And Let There Be Light

Your lighting impacts the atmosphere as well. You could choose to keep the light focused on you and keep your background in shadow, where the audience will barely be able to discern what is behind you. This allows you to be the center of focus, but it also shows that you are inside a room. Take a look at the channel VisualPolitik. Notice how you have the impression that the person is talking to you, but he is still present within an enclosed space. You cannot see the area, but if the presenter used a plain background, then the video might seem rather dull.

Objects in the background give more visual cues, keeping the brain occupied and the viewer interested. Furthermore, keeping the environment slightly in shadow ensures that the audience does not get too distracted by it and lose their focus on you and the primary message you are providing with your video.

Creating a YouTube video does involve a lot of thought, doesn't it? Well, that is how you make sure you have quality content.

And now, we shift the focus from you to your audience. Particularly, your followers.

Understanding YouTube's Improved Features

As the years pass by, more and more features are added to the platform. Let's examine some of those features that you might find useful for your channel.

Improved Comments

Comments are always welcome. You might get positive comments and then you might receive negative ones too. As a YouTube creator, you must be prepared to deal with both types of content. However, sometimes you might find out that there are junk comments added to your comments section. You might notice unwanted promotions or people simply spamming your comments section. In order to curb the spread of such content, YouTube has created a special ranking system. This new ranking system was created to reduce the visibility of junk comments and allow the creators to have a cleaner layout. This update has allowed content creators to make sure that they can keep their comment sections clean and safe for their audience.

Easier Access to Subscription Feed

The subscription feed is an important feature for creators. It allows the creators to know just who is watching their content and how much of the content is being consumed. By making it easy for creators to access their subscription feed, the platform has allowed for better understanding of user statistics. Plus, it becomes faster for you to simply head over to YouTube on your mobile phone to check your subscriber activity quickly.

Creator Community

Want to collaborate with other creators? All you have to do is join the Creator Community and then chat with fellow YouTubers. This allows you to come up with awesome collaboration ideas. You can find YouTubers who share your interests and think about producing content with them. Most YouTubers support each other by appearing in each other's videos. This degree of connectivity allows you to build your brand and improve your connections. No longer are YouTube creators alienated from each other, regardless of where they are in this world. The platform offers a whole new level of connectivity that is convenient and fun.

Chapter 4:
Growing Your Followers

Once you have confirmed the type of content you would like to push out, it is time to pay attention to your followers.

According to Google, YouTube has reached more than 2 billion monthly visitors in the fourth quarter of 2018. The tech giant also reported that the number of channels with more than 1 million subscribers has doubled in just 2018 itself.

Here is the best part; the number of YouTubers and vloggers who earn anywhere from $10,000 to $1million increased by 40%!

YouTube has become a global business brand, and people are now aware of its opportunity.

With that awareness comes the avidity for people around the world to start their own YouTube channel. As the video sharing platform has shown us that it can make almost any type of content popular, people have realized that they can create their own brand on the platform based on their interests

This indicates two significant things:

- What are you waiting for? It is time for you to get started and be part of an online content community; a community that can make money through their interests or passion.

- Joining YouTube means joining the ranks of hundreds of

content creators in your chosen niche alone. That means competition. That means you need to know how to get your audience better than your competition.

So where do you get started? Fortunately, I have some tips for you.

- The first thing I would like to emphasize is your schedule. If you are going to push out your content every Thursday, then make sure you stick to that timeline. A robust program allows your audience to expect your next video. When they know that you are regular, they follow you. If they feel that you publish your content whenever you can, they have no incentive to support you.

- Use keywords to optimize your video. I have a whole section dedicated to keywords under Chapter 6. We will run through some techniques where we reach that section.

- Ask your viewers to like, subscribe, and comment on your videos. These prompts are a way to enforce the message that your audience should start following you. If you can, talk about why they should continue supporting you. You can keep it something short like, "If you like this video, do not forget to hit like and leave a comment below. Click on the subscribe button and the bell icon for more great content! Again, this is XYZ; signing off!"

- Try to see if you can collaborate with other YouTubers to promote your content. You could approach those who have the same number of followers as you do.

- Keep engaging with your fans. During the initial phase, respond to the comments on your channel, drop in a like wherever you can, and address some queries in your video. Speak to those fans who engage with your video frequently. They are your loyal followers. You can directly ask them to shares your videos, bring in more followers or even get more views.

- When you start pushing out more content, remove previous material that you feel are not up to your current standards. Furthermore, this keeps your channel clean and relevant.

- YouTube is a community. Moreover, a community often engage in conversations. One of the ways you can develop your channel is to comment on other videos. Show your support. Give valuable feedback. Do not just leave a comment promoting your channel. For example, if you have a gaming channel, then seek out other gamers on YouTube. Head over to their channel and watch their content. Then leave a genuine response to their video. What did you think of their opinion? Have you tried out the video game that they are referring to in their video? Do you have a comparison to make between two games or products? Once you do, leave a comment giving a short line about your channel.

  - Make use of the new notifications feature for subscribers. Ask your community to click on a special 'bell' shaped button. The benefit to using the button is that every time you upload a video, your subscribers will be immediately notified of it. This allows them to head over to your video and watch it. The more they watch your videos, the more your videos will appear on the "Recommended Section" of a user's YouTube page. In other words, YouTube automatically promotes your videos the more views it gets. Use this to your advantage. If you have to, use the last or first part of the video to inform your audience to subscribe to your videos and click on the 'bell' icon to keep them notified of your content.

When using social media channels, try the below tips:

- Create your Facebook page and then publish your video directly to Facebook. Do not post a link of your YouTube video. This is because Facebook as an auto-play feature. You might have noticed this yourself. As you are scrolling your Facebook feed, you might come across a video that begins to play automatically. To take advantage of this feature, post your video on Facebook natively. Include a text in your post talking about your YouTube channel, encouraging the user to subscribe to your videos. You could also post your YouTube video links into the post text (after you upload the video).

- If you would like to promote your YouTube channel on your Facebook page, then you should boost your Facebook page as well. Here are a few ways to do it without spending on Facebook ads:

  - Ask your friends and family to follow you and share your content as much as possible. See if they are willing recommend you to other people as well.

  - Put a link in your YouTube page. This might sound somewhat counter-intuitive. After all, you are promoting your YouTube channel via Facebook by posting your Facebook page link on your YouTube? Something seems wrong about that. However, here is the reason for it. When you get more people on your Facebook, and they start following you, then your content appears on their feed. Even more, this means that their friends, in turn, get to see your content. That said, this eventually leads to more significant exposure and you know the rest. Think of it this way; there were 2.83 billion people on Facebook in the fourth quarter of 2018. There is so much potential in that number.

- Use your Facebook page to highlight more about your content. Post behind-the-scenes images and videos, talk about upcoming shows, ask the viewers to pick a topic between two options, and more. With the ability to use different kinds of content of Facebook, you can market your video channel effectively.

- Brand your Facebook page in a way that is consistent with your YouTube page. People need to be able to recognize you easily on both platforms.

- Maintain consistent updates on your Facebook page as well. That said, you do not want to create a page and neglect it.

- You can use Instagram to promote your channel. Here are some ways to do it:

  - As with your Facebook page, keep your Instagram updated regularly.

  - Make use of hashtags on Instagram. Find out the most popular using free online tools such as TagBlender and HashtagForLikes. You can look for the most popular hashtags on Instagram or even discover trending hashtags based on a specific category. Using a combination or generally popular hashtags and category specific tags allows you to reach a wider audience effectively.

- Post the link of your latest video on your Instagram profile. As soon as you update your profile, upload a post that mentions the link and encourage users to click-through.

- Make sure that you brand your Instagram photos. This way, if your images get re-shared, people will know about you.

- Add a little extra on Instagram. Throw in a few exclusive clips or images of your content. You could share a teaser image of your upcoming content, give a glimpse of your personal life, or tour of your studio. Do remember that you do not have to share every moment of your own life. You have to share something that allows your audience to see your personality. Perhaps you could give them a book recommendation, maybe take a picture at your favorite food joint, or perhaps a shot of you excited about an upcoming movie.

- As with any social channel, interact with your Instagram followers. Answer questions, start conversations, share tips, and just enjoying talking to your audience. Users will automatically begin to respond to you and eventually, recommend you to their friends.

Getting an Agency

If you are finding it difficult to juggle different aspects of your YouTube marketing, then you could consider getting in touch with a marketing agency. Remember that each agency has its price, targets, methods, and team of experts. Likewise, this means that each agency will approach your YouTube channel from a different perspective.

Along with the pricing that each agency charges you, think about the following options to make an informed decision in choosing an agency:

- Flexible: You need to find an agency that can adapt the latest trends, technology, and techniques to market your YouTube channel. They need to have the flexibility to work around changes, rather than sticking to one avenue of strategy and refusing to alter their methods.

- Adaptability: The agency needs to adapt to your channel. One cannot use the same marketing strategies for all YouTube channels. Since you are starting, you might have your own goals, schedules, content, target audience, and many other criteria. A good agency will analyze all these criteria and create a custom strategy to fit your channel specifically.

- Knowledge: Most important, the agency should know what they are doing. That said, this means having experience of the platform that they are working on. They should be able to give your answers to your queries. They should be able to alleviate your doubts. Having an agency that takes half-measures does not help you in any way. You might as well do the job yourself.

- Transparency: No process is perfect. Even if the strategy

is built on solid research and ideas, it may not work sometimes. Marketing is a trial and a test process. When one approach does not work, others are available. However, you should always be kept in the loop about the agency's activities. Whether they have good news or bad, you have the right to know.

- Vision: Finally, the agency should have a clear vision for marketing your channel. Directly bringing together different strategies in the hope that it might boost your channel does not guarantee success.

Tools of The Trade

If you do not have the budget for an agency, you could use online platforms and software. There are many tools available online that can help you market your content on YouTube effectively. The list below includes a combination of free and paid tools.

Let us look at some of them:

YouTube Studio

First and foremost, you need to stay updated about your channel. Which means, you should be able to access your channel's insights, video comments, playlists, and other features on the fly.

To take advantage of this convenience, you need YouTube Studio, a tool used by almost every YouTube vlogger, whether they are beginners or professionals. The strength of the tool is that you can download it as an app straight into your phone.

You can use YouTube Studio to monitor your videos, check their performance, and respond to comments. You can even make small changes – such as changing your video description, modifying thumbnails, creating schedules, and more – to your video wherever you are. You can also choose to turn on push notifications for your videos.

Social Blade

Would you like to know how your competitors are performing? Then look no further than Social Blade. The tool gives you a rundown of your YouTube channel, showing you details such as the number of subscribers you have gained, video views, and even estimated earnings per day. You can make a daily comparison of your YouTube channel and work with them to improve your marketing strategy. Apart from that, it also allows you to tap into your competitor's channels. You get to find out about their subscriber count, videos views and estimated earnings as well.

This information is useful because it allows you to find out what your competition is doing right. Do they have better video quality? Are they publishing content more frequently? Furthermore, are they promoting their channel better?

TubeBuddy

One of the reasons this tool is popular is because it can be launched directly from your browser. TubeBuddy is a browser extension, which removes the process of running a software every time you open your YouTube channel.

The convenience of the tool lies in the fact that you can run tests on various components of your channel. You can use the tool to test tags, titles, thumbnails, and even descriptions.

It gives you analytics on your tests, allowing you to make informed decisions about your content. You can also use the tool to schedule your videos or even remove them at a specific date and time.

You can upload videos in bulk using the tool. This is perfect if you have completed creating multiple videos. You can upload them all together and then put a schedule for each one. Even more, this saves you from the time-consuming process of uploading each video separately. Additionally, once you have added your videos, you can perform content tests on each video.

Canva

Need help creating thumbnails? Then you can head over to Canva and look at many design options. You can pick your background or upload an image from your computer. You can change the color tone of the image and add text and graphics. Canva will automatically show you how your image will appear on various platforms.

The software is perfect for beginners to get started. Until you have the perfect idea for your thumbnail, you can begin with Canva to get a YouTube brand for yourself.

Bitly

When you want to use links to your YouTube videos or your Facebook page, you might find yourself with a rather long URL. Shortening the URL allows you to keep your content clean. If there are character restrictions, then a short URL will take minimal space. This is where Bitly comes in. The tool creates short versions of your link that you can use anywhere.

Additionally, you can also use Bitly to check the analytics of your links. You can see how many people clicked-through using the link as each one of them features Bitly's UTM parameters.

You are now ready to market your YouTube channel. Remember that consistency is the key and there is no solid strategy to follow. Use every tool available to you and ensure you keep your eyes on your analytics. Data allows you to work with your content and make the right decisions.

Building Your Brand

Over 1 billion hours of videos are watched every day on YouTube.

Everyday.

Think about that statistic for a bit and realize how much potential you have to create a brand that is recognizable and memorable.

Today, we are in the age of YouTube Originals, where creators produce episodic series and publish them on YouTube. It goes to show just how much influence the channel has on people and the way they consume content.

So how can you create a brand? What is necessary to make it influential? How do you promote it? These are some of the questions I will approach in this chapter.

100% Authentic

How do you create an authentic brand? What should you do to maintain that brand image and make it profitable?

One of the most critical factors that you have to consider is how your brand will represent you. Your channel is an extension of your interest, passion, and even personality. Those elements are vital in creating a brand that you will be happy to promote.

A lesson in branding could come from the channel

WhatCulture. They have their style of creating instantly recognizable content. You could remove the opening sequence, and you can still identify their video.

What makes them so noteworthy and unforgettable?

They know their audience.

You cannot target everyone with your videos. There will always be people who may not wish to watch your video. However, that is okay — your goal to grab the attention of those who are likely to be interested in your content.

To do that, you need to consider a few points.

What kind of content would your audience appreciate?

Let us say that your videos are going to focus on car reviews. In this scenario, you should ask if your audience would appreciate serious content or get behind something more humorous.

If you are unsure how to answer this question, then look to your competitors. Top Gear is an example that you could consider. They have millions of followers, and their videos are fun, quirky, and adventurous.

Is that something you would like to consider?

Do note that when I say serious content, I don't mean you should not have a personality. If you are a car reviewer, then you need to have a charismatic demeanor while showing enthusiasm for cars.

Use the About Section

Your YouTube channel features an about section that allows you to add in some details about you and your channel. Many people navigate to this section to know more about you and your content. Please do not leave this section blank or fill it out carelessly. Put some thought into what you want your audience to read in this section.

You want to combine an introduction to yourself with highlights about what people can expect from your content. You could also add in your schedule and social media links.

Do not miss any opportunity to promote yourself, no matter how insignificant you think it is.

Research Your Competition

At any point in your content creation, you should avoid plagiarizing your content. However, that does not mean you cannot extract style, presentation, set-up, lighting, atmosphere, and other ideas from your competitors. Ideally, look to content creators of your niche and see what works. Discover the type of content that is popular with the audience and put your spin on it.

Using Live Streams

It is now easier to post live streams. Entertainment, gaming, learning and many other kinds of content creators are part of the delivery system. Gone are the lengthy setups and applications that you might have to use in order to get a livestream done properly. Now you can easily start streaming with a few simple steps. Do you want to start interacting with your audience about a topic? No problem. Want to stream a video of you cooking or creating something while keeping your audience engaged? You sure can! The ability to stream easily opens up new avenues for content. When the audience realizes that they are going to be part of a content creator's video experience, it gets them even more excited to come and watch the video.

More Content. More Love!

YouTube is trying to divert away from one-off content and viral hits. That means that if you truly want to create viral content, then you need to show YouTube that you are a content creator who spends a lot of time on the platform. A year ago, people could create viral content and when it hit millions of views, they could sit back and continue to enjoy the income gained from the video.

Not today. You need to put in the effort and make sure that you are keeping your channel active in order to enjoy the fruits of your labor. If YouTube discovers that you have not been keeping your account active, it will immediately start removing advertisements from your videos. This doesn't mean that you have to create videos every day. What I mean is that you can't just create content and then stop doing anything to your channel for a year or more. You need to keep the wheels of your content churning.

Additionally, YouTube wants to build a large network of creators. This means that once you start building your channel, look to partner with other channels as well. It doesn't matter if the other channel is small or big. What matters is that you have a network of content creators. That way, you build audiences faster and YouTube loves you for that!

Chapter 5:
Ranking Your Videos

YouTube has a robust algorithm that runs through every video to find out its performance. How well your video does decides how high your channel will be ranked on YouTube. As I had mentioned before, if your video does not bring in views and engagement, you will find your content dropping in the rankings.

So what do you do to boost your rankings?

Simple, you perform SEO for your content.

Of course, you might think that SEO is meant only for Google search results. However, YouTube is also a form of search engine that requires you to work on your content to optimize your content to rank better.

So let us see the many ways to optimize your content and more specifically, finding and using keywords in your YouTube videos.

Discovering Keywords

The first element that you should focus on is your keywords. When you have made the decision to research your keywords, you can approach the process in many ways.

You can utilize search results

If you head over to YouTube, then some of the high-ranking

videos incorporate their keywords within their titles. For example, if a movie channel is discussing the ending of a movie, they usually go with titles like "The Ending of [Movie] Explained!]" or "Understanding [Movie] Ending."

What the creators of the video are doing is incorporating the popular search terms into the title itself.

There are a couple of ways to discover the right keyword.

You can head over to the YouTube search bar, start typing a phrase, and note the search suggestions that appear. YouTube uses these recommendations because they are the top performing search results.

Why does YouTube recommend only the best?

Simple. It wants you to watch videos that have better average watch time. Furthermore, this means that the likelihood of you staying on the video and finding it interesting is high. YouTube obviously wants you to consume more content. What better way than to take you the high-ranking ones?

For example, if you are a travel vlogger and you are about to focus your video on Singapore's best tourist spots, then this is what you should do.

- Type in "Singapore tourist" in YouTube's search bar

- Note the first three search recommendations provided by YouTube. For example, they could be "Singapore tourist attractions," "Singapore tourist visa," and "Singapore tourist places."

- Out of the three results mentioned above, only two relate to your content. Those two would be "Singapore tourist attractions" and "Singapore tourist places."

- Now you need to figure out how to use these keywords into your title. Some of the options that you can use for your claim could be along the lines of "10 Best Singapore Tourist Places" or "Your Guide to the Best Singapore Tourist Attractions."

Another way to find out keywords is to perform a Google search. Try using a combination of different keywords into the search results of Google.

Taking the example of the Singapore tourist video that we discussed above, try using various queries related to your content into Google.

You could perform searches using the following queries:

- Singapore tourist guide

- Singapore tourist locations

In the search results that appear, you should be able to notice a YouTube video result among the various website suggestions.

Note down the title of the YouTube video. Let us assume that it says 7 Top Tourist Attractions in YouTube.

You now have an idea of how your YouTube title should be like. You could work around the Google search result and then use titles such as:

- Top Tourist Attractions in Singapore

- Top 6 Tourist Attractions to Visit in Singapore

- Your Best Guide to Tourist Attractions in Singapore

This way, you allow Google to make a recommendation for you. Knowing that Google prioritizes the best links in its search results, you can be confident that the title you are working with has many click-throughs.

If you cannot find a video result in Google search, then look or the "Video" tab right below the search bar. Click on it to get results for video and then scroll down to see the first two or three YouTube video results.

If there are no more than one YouTube result on the first page of Google, then you could note down the title of that video and use a different query for your search.

This way, you can get multiple options to work with.

Use a Keyword Tool to Get the Best Results

One of the tools that I recommend is Kparser. You can use the tool for free, but you will have to pay to take advantage of the advanced features.

With this tool, you can conduct searches specifically for YouTube and even look through your results based on country. The language options give you a nice little addition to browse through keywords in different languages, should you decide to push out content in your native language.

In the search results, you will notice keywords have rankings based on the frequency of each keyword being used in titles. On the left, you will also see a tab that shows you related keywords that you can base your search on.

Another tool that you could use is Wordtracker. The best part is that you can choose to get started on the tool using a trial period. If you are satisfied with its functionalities, you can choose to upgrade your plan.

Both the options that I mentioned above have affordable

payment options so you might not be shelling out a significant amount to use their features.

Add in a Plugin to Your Browser

You could make use of plugins that allow you to discover the keywords used in a particular video.

A popular tool that you can use for this is Tags for YouTube or TubeBuddy (which I talked about before).

With these tools, you can head over to the description section of the video and notice the keywords that appear. These are all the keywords that are used by your competitor.

The best part? These tools are free to use!

Let's Play Tag!

Now it is time to optimize your tags.

- Head over to your profile icon and click it, choosing the "My Channel" option from the drop-down menu that follows.

- In the next page, head over to "Channel Settings"

- Now click on the "Info and Settings" option

- You will not be able to see a "Tags" field, where you can enter your preferred tags

I recommend four types of tags that you can use for your video:

- Content Tags: These are tags that pertain to your content. Once, again, taking the Singapore tourist example, your tags should be as listed below:

  - Singapore

- Singapore tourist places/Singapore tourist locations

- Singapore tourist attractions

- Singapore guide

- Subject Tags: You use these tags based on the subject matter of your content. So, continuing with our example, our topic is based on tourism and tourist guides. That said, let us go ahead and use some of the tags of this category:

  - Tourist guides

  - Tourism

  - Travel guides

  - World travel

- Broad Tags: These are tags that are closely related to your subject matter but are still relevant for the search engine. These help you grab as much audience as possible. For our example, the tags would be as shown below:

- Travel

  - Asian countries

  - Asian cuisine (if you have food content in your video)

  - Parks (if you have parks included in your video)

- Error Tags: I like to use these tags in case people make errors when typing out a keyword. These are the tags you intentionally spell wrong so that YouTube has a wider combination of words to work with. Here are some examples:

- Singapore

- Travel

- Guides

- Tourist

To work with each of the above tags, use your keyword tool to find out the best combinations. For example "Tour guide" might be ranked as a better keyword than "Tourist guide." If that is indeed the case, then you are better of using Tour Guide as your tag.

Edit Your Closed Captions

You might have seen this option on YouTube videos. It is usually at the bottom right of the video with the initials "CC."

If you turn on this option, you will notice that captions appear on the video. These captions are primarily used for those who are deaf or who have hearing problems.

What many people do not realize is that as the closed captions include content, they can be crawled by Google (a.k.a. YouTube). While the priority given to the closed captions are not high, it is still a slight boost to your video's ranking.

YouTube automatically provides captions to your videos. However, I would recommend editing them often; the captions are not always right and do not work with all accents.

To edit your captions, head over to your profile and enter Creator Studio.

- Once here, click on the "Video Manager" tab.

- Choose the video you want to add captions to and then click on Edit

- In the drop-down menu that follows, choose Subtitles and CC.

- You will notice caption tracks for your video. Look at them and click on the one you would like to edit.

- You can now click on any line in the caption and edit the content.

- Once you have made the changes, click "Save."

Add Your Description

This part of your content is vital for your ranking. You can play around with your description because you get a lot of space to describe your content and enter your keywords.

You get to use up to 5,000 words in your description. That gives you enough content to enter a few details and here is what I recommend:

The first few lines appear in the search results of YouTube. So make sure it is attractive, includes your main keyword, and short. Make it snappy and try to entice the viewer.

The first three lines will be visible under your video without having to click the "See More" option. Make use of this to encourage your audience to click more.

Add in as many details of your video after the first few lines. Give your audience a taste of what they can expect from the content without giving away too much. After all, you do want to watch the video. For example, if your content is focused on the top ten beauty products of 2018, then let your audience know that your video will focus on a top ten beauty products list. However, do not give away what beauty products you will be covering in your video. That way, your viewers already have all the information they need and might not watch your video.

Add in your social links. If you have a Facebook, Twitter, Instagram, Pinterest or even blog page, make sure you add those links in the description.

If you have a page where you are selling merchandise, include a link to that page here as well.

Ensure that you sprinkle your keyword through the description two or three times. Do not repeat the keyword more than three times or YouTube might consider the content as spam and demote your video.

Finally, add a link to your channel as well so that you have more chances to send people to your content.

Remember to use Bitly for all links. This way, you can keep track of the number of people who have clicked-through using your links. By using Bitly, you can notice if your links are attracting clicks. If they are not, then perhaps you could place them higher in the description and see the results. Alternatively, you can see if the content in the description is not attractive enough. Whatever the conclusion you draw, Bitly helps you monitor the effectiveness of the link placements in your description.

View From the Top

Getting views is how people become aware of your content, share it with their friends and family, comment on your channel or even subscribe to your videos. So how can you derive more views from YouTube users? Let me show you a few ways you can accomplish this.

When in Doubt, Ask Your Audience

Who better to understand what your viewers are interested in watching than the viewers themselves? When you are starting out, try to get your audience to choose what they would like to see next. You could do this in many ways.

Look through the comments sections. You might be able to gain valuable inspiration from the conversations and debates taking place there.

Alternatively, you can give options at the end of your video.

For example, if you have a cooking channel, then you could end the video by asking your audience what they would like you to prepare next. Give them an option between two sweet dishes or two quick-meals.

In similar ways, you can explore tons of content by simply looking to your audience for insights.

Get Social

As I mentioned previously in this chapter, begin promoting your YouTube page on Facebook and other social channels. Find any number of opportunities to spread the word about your content. Is Snapchat popular in your region? Open a Snapchat account and get busy. Is Twitter preferable? Then make sure you are on the channel. Pinterest? Tumblr? Whatever options are available to you, make sure you exhaust them. After all, you might as well do it right the first time.

Add a Watermark to Your Video

Other than having an end screen, make sure that you are using watermarks and graphics in your video. You might have to use video editing software to accomplish this, or you could use the help of an accomplished video editor. You could always refer to the platforms I had mentioned under the "Getting Someone to Create Your YouTube Channel" section to find someone with the skills to work on your task. Using a watermark, you can place a permanent "Subscribe" icon in your video itself. That said, this is an excellent way to encourage your audience to subscribe to your channel and increase views on upcoming videos.

Using graphics, you can add a small animation that pops up and lets the audience know to subscribe to your channel. Once again, you could create a graphic for yourself or hire someone to do the job. Remember that the graphic should appear once during your video if your video is less than 15 minutes. That said, this is also to ensure that it does not interrupt the viewing experience. Your audience might get the impression that you are trying too hard to get them to follow your channel. Furthermore, this is a poor impression to place on your audience, especially when you want them to engage more with your content.

Important Things to Note

- Make sure that you are watching other videos on YouTube. One of the tricks that you can use is to go over to the trending section of YouTube and see what topics the videos are focusing on. For example, let's say that there is a new movie everyone is excited about. People are starting to create content regarding that topic. Why not use that opportunity to make your own unique content on that topic?

• Once you have created your content of the trending topic, use the topic itself as the keyword for your videos. For example, let's say that the trending topic is about keto diet and you have created content based on that topic, make sure that the word "keto diet" appears in the title of your video and the video description. Follow this rule for any type of content. Make sure that the content-related keyword is included in the video's title and description.

• Avoid content related to sensitive topics and definitely avoid using marked keywords. This is a sure way to get your video demonetized. However, if you are creating an opinion related video, then you might want to use your best judgment when creating your content. One of the best pieces of advice that I can give you is to create a script that you can use for your video. Fine-tune the script based on the latest YouTube guidelines. It's not easy to find information about YouTube directly on the platform. I strongly recommend following the channel "YouTube Analyzed" to get more info about the platform and its ever-shifting guidelines. On that channel, you can get an entire list of words that you should watch out for and how to properly (and safely) create content for your channel.

• Before you upload your video, check the content and edit it properly. Keep the video interesting and free of explicit content. Even an accidental addition could cost you monetization features.

• Make sure that you are not using copyrighted material. YouTube can detect such materials even if you use less than 7 seconds worth of copyrighted content. If you really have to use it, you can either edit the audio to add in your own audio track or submit an appeal to YouTube itself to explain the necessity for adding the content in your video. Alternatively, you can get in touch with the owner(s) of the content and request their permission to use them.

• Be attentive to your community. Do not ignore their feedback. Do not ignore the negative feedback as well. Whatever the community says about your video is an opportunity for you to improve the content of your channel, and increase views.

• Be careful when you open emails that claim that they are from brands or businesses. If you get emails from people who claim that they want to advertise on your channel, make sure that you contact them directly to get more information on the promotion. Sometimes, you might be a victim of a scam. When you click on dangerous links, hackers can easily take over your YouTube account and block you from using your own account!

Chapter 6:
Monetizing Your Content

After going through the steps to find your niche, setting up your YouTube, creating your content, and even finding ways to market your videos, we have reached this section; how to make money through your YouTube channel. To get the dough rolling into your account, it will require you to continually work on your content while using various means to monetize your account. Let us get started with the below.

Affiliations

If your channel uses products in its videos (which typically happens with most YouTube content), then users might be enticed into purchasing those very same products. You can always link your viewers to the products page and encourage them to get the products for themselves. By doing this, you get a commission for every purchase that is made through your channel. The logic behind this commission structure is that you are promoting the product on your channel, giving it greater visibility, and get a small portion of the sale.

Amazon Affiliates is one of the most popular affiliate platforms that you can take advantage of for your channel. It is easy to configure with Amazon, and you will be provided with a unique affiliate link that you can use in the description of your videos.

A few points to remember when you are using these links:

Product Reviews

One of the best ways to use affiliate links is through product review videos. This way, you can link the audience to the product page without your audience wondering why you have included the link. Let us take an example. If you had a travel video in which you used the latest DSLR from Canon for capturing the shots, it might not be wise to add a link to the product page. This is because you are not directly reviewing the product.

When your audience notices this, they might get the impression that you have lost the authenticity in your videos. They might imagine that you created the content merely to promote a product or brand.

However, what you can do is create a separate video to educate your audience on how you create your travel videos. In this video, you can explain the different techniques and products you use to create your videos. You could then provide product links in the description.

Keep in mind that you should do this if you notice positive feedback from your audience. There is no point on creating an informative video about your content if your audience has not asked for it.

Getting Affiliates

You do not have to stick to just Amazon. Some of the other significant affiliate programs that I can recommend are:

- eBay Partners

- ShareASale Affiliates

- Rakuten Marketing Affiliates

- Shopify Affiliate Program

Each platform has its own setup process, so make sure to go through the details for each individual program to better understand how you can get started with affiliate marketing.

Linking It

When you have successfully collaborated with an affiliate platform, you will be given product links that you can use on your YouTube channel.

Just a tip from my end; you can use the same link on multiple platforms. So let us say that you have a Facebook, Twitter, and Instagram account, you can put the product link in all these platforms. Every sale that you make through these platforms gives you a portion of the sale. The more links you place on your social platforms, the more sales you can make.

Cloak Your Links

One of the things that you should do is to cloak your affiliate links. This is because the link URL might give out information about where to get the product. Using this information, your audience can purchase the product directly from the website instead of using the link in your description.

I recommend using Bitly for cloaking your links. There are two reasons for this:

- You can create short links easily and no one will be able to see where the link takes them

- You will be able to track the clicks on the links, allowing you to see if their placement in your description section is effective.

Limit the Number of Links You Use

Finally, do not go overboard with the number of affiliate links you use under your videos. YouTube has a strict policy that might lead to a ban on your channel if you use too many links. That said, this is because YouTube wants their audience to stay on the platform longer. Linking to external sources means that you are taking users to another platform.

Getting Paid By Views

Have you noticed those ads that appear on YouTube as soon as you play a video? Well, YouTube pays the channel that plays that advertisement.

That is right.

Ads are how YouTube makes money and why they offer so many free services. However, they do not show ads on just any channel. You need to generate regular content to become part of the YouTube Partner Program, or YPP for short, which allows you to generate revenue through ads.

With this program, you allow various marketers to show their ads through your channel. Ads are based on a pay-per-view scheme. Moreover, this means that YouTube considers these ads viewed by the audience only if a user watches the advertisement for a specified period.

To become part of the program your channel needs to meet the below criteria:

- The channel needs to have at least 1,000 subscribers

- You need to have gained at least 4,000 watch hours on your channel

Joining the YPP

To become part of the Partner Program, go will first through the below steps:

- Go over to your profile icon and then enter Creator Studio

- Once you are in Creator Studio, head over to the Channel tab

- On the page that follows, click on Status and Features

- Finally, go to the Monetization option and then click on Enable

YouTube will then take your account through a verification process. Once the platform approves your channel, you will officially be a YouTube Partner.

Selling Your Branded Items

Once you have cultivated a reputation on YouTube and start attracting views, you can also put your brand on items. Some of the most common issues that feature the brands of channels are t-shirts, mugs, pens, and other small items. With your brand, you can sell your merchandise on YouTube. In fact, the platform has made it easier for you to promote your branded goods. You can now have a single row of items displayed below your video, allowing the audience to directly check out your merch and make a purchase if they want to. Purchases will be made through your website. Every time someone clicks on an item, they will be directed to your site where they can buy the item.

To enable this option, you will need to meet the criteria established by Google. These are:

- You should be part of the YouTube Partner Program. To know the requirements to be part of the program, check out the "Getting Paid By Views" section.

- You should have more than 10,000 subscribers

- Your channel had no Community Guideline Strikes. Google gives you a strike if you break their community guidelines. Make sure you are aware of these guidelines and know how to avoid receiving any penalty.

If your channel meets the criteria, you can allow YouTube to place a "Merchandise Shelf" on your channel. To do this, follow the steps as listed below:

- Head over to your profile and then navigate to Creator Studio.

- Click on the Monetization tab

- Select the Merchandise option. This option will be automatically available to you if you meet all of Google's criteria.

- Finally, follow the instructions given to you to add the Merchandise Shelf option, allowing you to display your products under your video.

With the option enabled, you can add up to twelve items to be displayed below your video.

Do note that only four or five items will appear under your video on the desktop version of YouTube and only one item will appear on the mobile version.

Selling the Products of Others

You can use your channel for marketing another brand's or individual's products. Furthermore, this is a great way to form business relationships and partnerships with others while also earning a little commission from the sale of their products. There are many ways you can accomplish this:

If they have their product listed on Amazon, then you can make use of Affiliate Marketing to promote their products on your channel. To make use of Affiliate Marketing, refer to the section "Getting Affiliates."

If they do not have their products listed anywhere, then you could give a mention of their products on your channel. Be advised; it should appear as native as possible. Merely talking about someone else's products might not sit well with your audience.

If it is a branded product and your channel's niche relates to the product category, then you could give a product review. For example, if you are a tech channel and Oppo, the mobile phone manufacturer, reaches you, then you could consider reviewing their product. Do note that you should keep your channel's identity. This means that during the review, do not exaggerate the positives of the product to satisfy the client. Be honest about the review but give more mentions of some of the features that you like.

With these methods, you can efficiently market products from brands, businesses or even individuals.

The Added Value of Ads

Finally, you can use YouTube ads to promote products, brands, or even yourself. One of the most significant benefits of using

YouTube ads is the reach that they provide you. You can target a broad audience or reach out to a specific audience based on certain parameters. YouTube makes this process of reaching your audience possible through its targeting mechanics. You can reach out to people based on their demographics, locations, the platform (whether you prefer mobile or desktop audiences), audience interests, and even certain times of the day.

You can also set a start date and an end date for your YouTube ad. Even more, this allows you to monitor your budget and give your ads as much exposure as you can afford.

YouTube ads also allow you to measure their performance. This will enable you to make changes to the ads or stop the ad entirely if you so choose. This level of flexibility gives you greater control over your promotions.

With all of these features, you can discover the right way to advertise products, channels or specific videos. If you are an up and coming DJ and you have a YouTube channel, then you can promote your video to gain more exposure to your music. Similarly, if you have a brand you would like to advertise, you can create a short video for the brand and then use YouTube ads to send across the brand's message to an audience.

YouTube ads also allow you to interact with the viewers through responses, allowing you to monitor how effective your ads have been.

You might have seen different forms of ads on YouTube. While you might think that they are all the same, you should be aware of a few various styles of ads. There are a few primary types of ads on YouTube:

TrueView Ads

By using this form of ad, you as an advertiser will only pay for the advertisement if the audience watches at least 30 seconds, watch the entire ad or take action on the ad. These actions can be in the form of clicks made on the call-to-actions placed on the ad.

TrueView Ads can be further broken down:

Video Discovery Ads

You will notice these ads on the search result page. You may also spot them on the YouTube homepage or under the related videos column of your video. You will start noticing these ads after you perform a YouTube search.

In-Stream Ads

If you click into these ads, you will be taken to the video page of that ad. On the right-hand side of the page (if you are on a desktop), you will notice a display banner feature related videos of the channel.

Preroll Ads

These ads play before you begin to watch the video that you selected on YouTube. You might be aware of these ads; you can watch for five seconds and then you receive the option of skipping the ad.

With In-Stream Ads, you can add custom call-to-actions on the ad itself, allowing you to take the audience to a web page, social media page, or other locations.

Bumpers

The last form of an ad is Bumpers. These ads are gaining popularity across YouTube channels because of their concise length. These ads appear only before a YouTube video plays and last for just six seconds. While you might not have the flexibility to add as much messaging as possible into these ads, you must know that these ads extremely effective in communicating the message. That said, this is because as these ads are short, their limited messages are easy to digest and memorize.

With all this talk of ads, let us take a closer look at how you can set them up on your YouTube and run them effectively.

Partnering With Brands

Numerous YouTubers now partner with brands, that choose to advertise directly in the videos. This means that creators can talk about a product or service in their video.

The video starts off in the usual manner. The YouTuber starts talking about the video and describing its content. He or she then interrupts the video with a message from a 'sponsor,' who is the brand or business that the YouTuber has partnered with. The YouTube creator then introduces the product or service and highlights some of the most important features of the product. Once done, they go back to their regular video content.

This strategy is often employed by YouTubers who have sensitive content and are unable to monetize their videos directly through YouTube. Or it is also a method used by creators who do not create videos too regularly on YouTube in order to utilize the platform as an advertising medium.

Think about your channel and content. Then think about your goals for your channel. Would you prefer to use YouTube as your advertising partner? Or would you prefer to link directly with brands and businesses? The choice is yours and each option providea their own benefits.

When you partner with brands or businesses, then you can

enter into a direct contract with them. Anything you earn is based on the agreement that you created with the brand or business. YouTube does not take any percentage of the revenue that you earn. However, the amount that you earn depends on the brand you partnered with. You might not be able to advertise with big brands like Volkswagen, Pepsi, Microsoft, and others. You might mostly advertise the products of local businesses.

If you instead choose to partner with YouTube, then you receive the opportunity to advertise for various brands around the world. Depending on where your video is watched, the advertisements will be modified to link to the local brands. For example, if your video is being watched by people in Scotland, then you won't see advertisements of U.S. based businesses, unless those business entities have presence in Scotland or are specifically targeting the Scottish market.

Chapter 7:
Using YouTube Ads

YouTube ads are useful because they can visually create an impression in the minds of your audiences. I want to give you a rundown of how to create an effective YouTube ad. However, before that, let me get you started on how to get started with video ads.

AdWords

So the first step that you have to take before even thinking about the idea for your YouTube ad is to set up your Google AdWords account.

To set up your account, follow the below steps:

- Head over to the Google AdWords home page.

- Once there, you will neat to sign-up for a new account. If you already have Gmail, then you can use your mail to create an AdWords account.

- You will need to verify your AdWords account. If you had used your Gmail to create the account, then you can skip this step. That said, if you had to create an AdWords account from scratch, then you might have to complete the verification process. Furthermore, once you are done verifying your account, you can now start creating your YouTube Ads.

Creating Your First Campaign

As soon as you enter your AdWords account, you will notice an interface and some options on the left side of the screen. Select the "Campaigns" option. Once you reach this page, follow the below steps:

- Click on the "+" icon and then select the "New Campaign" option

- In the next page, you will notice a few options or ad goals. Not all of the options on the page allow you to create video ads. You should typically notice the below ad goals:

  - Sales

  - Leads

  - Website traffic

  - Product and brand consideration

  - Brand awareness and reach

  - App promotion

- Out of the above objectives, only the below goals allow you to use advertising on YouTube:

  - Leads

  - Website Traffic

  - Product and brand consideration

  - Brand awareness and reach

- Choose any of the above options that fit your requirements. As soon as you make a selection, you will have four options for campaigns. These are:

  - Search

  - Display

  - Shopping

  - Video

- Go ahead and select Video and then click on the "Continue" button

- Now you get to add more details about your campaign

Campaign Name

Go ahead and enter the name of your campaign. It does not have to be keyword friendly. You need to use a name for identification purposes.

Ad Format

Under this section, you get to choose between two options:

You can choose between "In-stream" form of ads, or you can select "Bumper" ads. You can decide which ad works for you based on your ad duration. If it is more than 6 seconds, then you should choose the "In-stream" ads. I would recommend getting started with this ad as you have better flexibility in terms of ad timings to send promotions to your audience.

Budget

When you have made your selection, put in your daily budget in the space provided. If you cannot figure out the amount you would like to out as your regular budget, then you could try this technique.

Plan out the total budget that you are willing to spend on YouTube ads. For the sake of this example, let us assume that you have a budget of $100 for the ads.

Not think of the duration of the ads. How long would you like to run them? Is it a particular time of the year (it could be the season, a specific festival or even a local event) that affects the duration of the ads? What is the goal you are trying to achieve?

Let us further assume that you have decided to run the ads for ten days.

In this case, you will be able to spend $10 every day. That amount becomes your daily spend.

When you have worked out your daily spend, go ahead and enter that number in the budget section.

Networks

Next, we will be looking at the systems you will use to promote your ads. You will get the option between YouTube Search and YouTube Videos networks.

Let us look at what these two options mean:

- YouTube Search

With this option, your video ads will appear in the search results. You will also be able to see them on the homepage and under the recommendations section.

- YouTube Videos

These refer to the TrueView ads and other forms of ads that

appear directly in the video, whether at the beginning, during video playback or at the end of the video.

If you feel conflicted when choosing between the two types of ads, then you could create one campaign for a YouTube Search ad and one for YouTube Videos ad. Let us get back to the budget example that we examined before. You have decided to use $10 ad a daily budget. However, now you would like to try out both the YouTube Search and YouTube Videos type of ads. All you have to do is split the budget again so that you will $5 to try out on each network types.

Here is a recommendation from my side; run the ads for a couple of days on the $5 budget and monitor them closely. At the end those two days, you might have a reasonably fair idea about which network yields better results for your ad. When you narrow down the best system for you, stop the other network. Now put the entire $10 into the network you have chosen as your preferred option.

Let us assume that YouTube Search works the best for you. You will stop YouTube Videos at the end of two days. For the remaining eight days of our campaign, YouTube search will run on a $10 daily budget.

Locations

Next, you can choose the areas where your ads will appear.

What does this mean? Say you are located in the Philippines and choose to use only the city of Manila as the location option. Your ad will only appear to those people who watch YouTube in Manila.

One of how you can choose the best location to target your ads is by heading back to YouTube Analytics.

If you are just starting out, you are probably popular in your home country. However, even if that is the case, find out if you are more fans from a particular city or region. Even more, this will help you reach to a maximum number of fans and help promote your brand effectively.

Language

You can select the language you would like to target. This option is excellent if you are not using ads in English.

Devices

In this section, you can choose the devices you would like to target. In the beginning, I would recommend not to touch this option. Google will automatically show your ads to all devices, whether they are connected to YouTube via a mobile phone, tablet or a computer. Advanced settings allow you to choose if you would like to target mobile users or include desktop audiences as well specifically. Additionally, you can choose to target people who use both WiFi and mobile networks or any one of the two.

You will notice another setting under Devices. This setting is labeled as "Set device bid adjustments."

What you can do here is increase or decrease the bid for a specific device by a percentage amount.

For example, you can choose to increase the bid by 50% for mobile devices. That said, this means that Google will increase the budget from $10 to $15 for mobile users. Of course, this means that you might have to spend a little more.

However, what you can also do is decrease the bid. Let us say that you would like to target mostly mobile phone users. So might choose to reduce the proposal for computer users by

50%. Meaning, Google will lessen the bid for computer users from $10 to $5.

Once again, I recommend not using these settings, as you might need plenty of data to modify them. Keep the settings in their default state for now.

Video Ad Creatives

Next, you will have the option to name your Ad Group. An Ad Group is merely a collection of ads that you would like to push on YouTube. Go ahead and give your Ad Group any name you want. Once you have chosen the title, you can then select the video that you would like to promote.

You can either search for the video directly or paste the URL of the video into the section provided.

If you chose In-Display ads, then you might have to ad in a Headline and two Descriptions as well. Go and fill those out. Make sure that your Headline features the main keyword that you are working with.

To find out what your main keyword is, think about the video that you are promoting. If it is a video about elements and their composition, then perhaps "Elements" should be your main keyword.

Add that into the Heading. For the above example, a few recommendations of Headings would be:

- Discover the Elements

- Think You Know Your Elements?

- Know More About The Elements

Remember that you can only use a maximum of 25 characters

for the title, so you have to be concise and clear about your message. Descriptions allow you to use up to 35 characters so once again, you have a little more room to work with, but you might still need to keep your messaging short and crisp. I would recommend keeping the Heading direct and straightforward. You could use a bit of creative fun with the Descriptions.

Bidding

You then put in the maximum amount that you would like to spend on each view. With your $10 budget, you could decide if you would like to spend up to $1 for each video or less. You could also choose to spend more. It is entirely up to you. Bear in the mind that when you set the maximum bidding amount, it does not mean that Google will spend $1 each time it shows the video. You are just defining the budget with which Google can work with. Moreover, this means that it could spend anywhere from $.1 to $1 per view, depending on where it is showing and who is watching the video.

Targeting

Now you get to choose your target audience. You can select the gender and age of your audience. You could also decide the parental status of the audience, in case you are targeting families or married people. You can choose to add in interests. Google has a comprehensive list of interests that you can select from.

Optional Targeting

You can also choose to target based on keywords or topics. For your first campaign, I would recommend running your campaign based on interests. There are multiple reasons for this:

- It is your first campaign, so you need to reach out to as many people as possible. This gives your channel and brand greater exposure.

- You need data for future campaigns, which is why you should consider your first YouTube campaign as merely a test run. The main reason for this is that at this point, you may not know how effective your ads are with specific audiences. Keeping a broad targeting option helps you derive some great insights from your ad campaign.

However, for subsequent campaigns, you could add in keywords as well. The best way to do this is by using the tools mentioned before.

Finally, you can complete your campaign and launch your ad.

Analyzing Your Ads

When you have finally launched your ad, head back to the main page of Google AdWords by clicking the "Campaign" tab.

Here, you will notice all the campaigns you are currently running. Now click on the most recent campaign you would like to look at. At this point, you might have only one campaign running; your test ad.

Once you enter the campaign, you will notice your ad set.

In the beginning, monitor these parts of your ad to get the best insights.

Views

You can use this metric to see how many views your ad received. If your ad is running successfully, you should usually see this number increasing daily. If the number drops for any reason, then you should consider changing your target or budget.

Likes and Shares

You can see the number of likes and shares the video received, allowing you to gauge audience engagement. You may not gain much engagement on your first ad, but that is okay. You are only getting started, and you may be able to use this campaign as a template to create better ads in the future.

Link Your YouTube and AdWords Account

Before you start making ads, you should link your YouTube account to your Google AdWords. To do this, you merely have to follow the below steps.

- Head over to YouTube's homepage

- From here, click on your profile icon and then choose Creator Studio

- In the options on the left, click oh Channel and then select the Advanced tab

- You will notice an option that says, "Google Ads account linking." Under this option, choose "Link a Google Ads Account"

- You will notice a set of instructions to follow

- Once you have completed the instructions, click on the "Finish" button

- Now head over to your Google Ads account

- You might have received a request to link your YouTube account

- Once you approved the request, your YouTube account and your AdWords are now linked

Using the Right Keywords

When you notice that your ads may not be performing as well as they should be, then you can make use of keywords to refine your ad. This way, you get to target only those audiences who are more likely to react to your ad and perhaps even engage with it.

For this, let us go ahead and see how we can find the right keyword.

Of course, the first option that you can use is to go right ahead and use the tools that I had recommended earlier.

However, another method is to use Google's Keyword Planner as well.

The first thing that you should do is find out your main keyword and then add an additional keyword. Do you remember the "Let's Play Tag!" section where we worked with creating different types of tags? Use the same option for your keywords as well.

Find four types of keywords for your ad.

Let us use an example to illustrate this.

For an ad that is focused on promoting your video focused on the history of Vikings, your ad breakdown should look something like the below.

Main Keyword

- Viking History

Content Keyword

These are keywords that directly link to your content and should look something like this.

- History of Vikings

- The Vikings

- Viking Facts

- Vikings Time Period

- Broad Keywords

- Viking People

Now you can start playing around with keywords to include those words or phrases that are useful to promote your video. Bearing this in mind, your keyword list might look something like this:

- History

- Scandinavian History

- Normandy

- Barbarians

- Cultures

For your YouTube ads, you do not need to choose keywords with misspellings. That said, this is because when you add keywords into Google, it automatically targets those search queries that have mistakes in them as well.

Now that you have your set of keywords head over to your Google Keyword Planner and then put your keywords in them.

Google will then provide your search results based on your keyword. In the page that follows, you will notice many columns, one of them being "Average Monthly Searches."

Look for your keyword and then look at the Average Monthly Searches is has received. If it is above 100, then you can go ahead and use the keyword. If the Average Monthly Searches is above 1,000, then that is even better, showing greater popularity for your keyword.

If the Average Monthly Searches is below 100, they consider one of the other keywords that Google recommends. These recommendations will appear right below your keyword. Look at ones that have more than 100 or 1,000 (or more if possible), and pick those. Add them to your keyword list.

With this method, you have a set of keywords that you can use for your video ad. Go ahead and add them to your ad. Then continue to monitor the progress of the advertisement after you have made the changes.

You should now be able to achieve better progress with your promotion.

Remember that you need to have a clear idea of what you want to achieve with your ad. If you are looking for more likes, then you should promote your video to as many people as possible. If you have a specific message to convey to your audience, then perhaps you could narrow down the targeting using keywords and ensure the right people see it. It is all up to you and how you would like to promote your content.

Conclusion

With that, we have come to the end of our educational journey to understanding YouTube.

There is so much you will learn on your own with regards to the content you are working with. You will discover how to improve your editing process. You may also gain more skills in creating lighting in your videos. Furthermore, you will also enhance your YouTube ad skills.

Whatever the scenario or area of focus, remember that working with YouTube is a consistent process. You may not see results immediately. Some YouTubers had to work for a few months before they noticed their content picking up.

Thankfully, YouTube is attracting more audience, so you are in the right phase of the video platform's growth to take full advantage of it, which is why you might not have to wait long to see the flow of traffic to your videos.

With that in mind, remember to keep your content consistent, find new ways to improve your videos, and always stay true to your style.

Good luck on your journey into branding yourself. I'm more than confident with a little consistency and practice, you too can have a moderate to even exceptional level of success!

12448165R00090